The Thread of Water

Ethnography, Photography, & Feminist Ecologies

JULIE PATARIN-JOSSEC

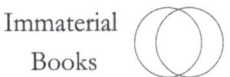

Immaterial
Books

First Edition 2024

Published by Immaterial Books
www.immaterialbooks.com

All images and text © Julie Patarin-Jossec

ISBN: 978-1-962415-00-2

Table of Contents

Acknowledgements   IX

Chapter 1: Plastic Lives   1
academia; ethics; ethnography; plasticity; trauma

Chapter 2: Flowing Bodies   15
diving; ecofeminism; embodiment; fluid; hydrofeminism

Chapter 3: Mythologies   31
commercial diving; gender; sexism; standard; techniques; technologies

Chapter 4: Colonial Scapes   45
colonialism; cosmologies; creativity; ecologies; exile; heat; indigeneity; industrialization; thermography

Chapter 5: Resilience   57
binding; oblivion; oceans; remembering; stars; salvation; water

Afterword: Following the Thread of Water   65
an essay by Greg Scott

ACKNOWLEDGEMENTS

All intellectual work has a plethora of influences and I could not stress enough how much this essay is a tributary of far more authors and theories than the few explicitly cited, for length and style. To all these theorists, artists and activists whose work has been a continuous inspiration, including Val Plumwood and Gloria E. Anzaldúa whose works are infused everywhere in my reflections.

To my cosmic friend Juan Francisco Salazar, who allowed this book project to surface.

To my colleagues and friends Gary Bratchford, John Grady, Susan Hansen and Kate Korroch, who supported me while I was sinking into the ocean depths.

To Brian O'Neill, whose dedication and passion has made this book possible.

To Greg Scott who, lucky me, revels in strangeness at least as much as I do.

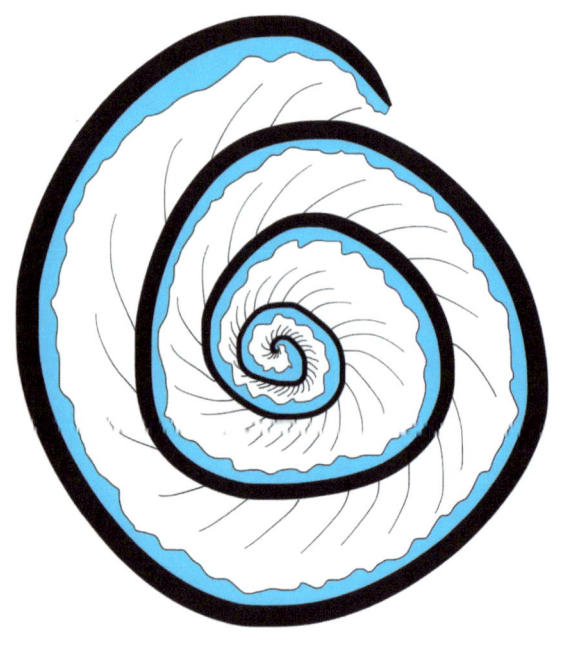

x

CHAPTER 1: PLASTIC LIVES

The plasticity of biological organisms is their ability to adapt and change when facing a new way of life.

Between 2018 and 2021, I exercised as a sociology lecturer at the State University of Saint-Petersburg, in Russia. My lectures were very much focused on ethnographic methodologies[1] and grounded in my own ethnography of the astronaut profession. At the end of June 2021, and the end of the academic year, I would have to leave Russia because most academic institutions were progressively interrupting all recruitment of foreign scholars in my field, among other political restrictions that didn't fit my convictions. I would have to throw away all the belongings that would not fit in my suitcases to leave the country – including most of the books I had used to write my dissertation – as in a symbolic au revoir to an obsolete version of me.

That was a semester before the War in Ukraine started.

While the plane bringing me back to France (where I was born, but felt I didn't belong) was flying over the Mediterranean coast, sea waves were reflecting sunlight through the window. This is all that it took to convince me I should try scuba diving. I had never dived in my life, and I barely enjoyed swimming – more because I never considered, or previously had an opportunity to experience, water as an element in which I would be especially comfortable.

And so I did: after a few days, I randomly picked a diving club and called to book a first dive. Twelve months later, I was certified as a technical diver

---

[1]. Ethnography is the social scientific method inherited from anthropology that has always profoundly shaped and defined my entire academic production. It is a qualitative method relying on the researcher's immersion within a community (i.e., the field).

in several categories, a commercial diver and a first-level scuba instructor. These certifications gave me the freedom to experiment with my practice in an unusual environment, and to own the way I exposed my body to the risk of hyperbaric exposure. These certifications did not mean I was not a scholar anymore – is it possible to stop being an ethnographer?

* * *

My commercial diver training lasted four months. It included all the activities and equipment that surface-supplied divers are likely to encounter in the course of their career:

> underwater welding;
> drilling and cutting with pneumatic and hydraulic tools;
> cutting with oxyacetylene torches;
> underwater pouring and demolding of concrete;
> object search;
> lifting and displacement using lifting bags and measured ropes;
> site cartography;
> localization and preparation of underwater sites (signposting);
> etc.

This led me to experience my surrounding environment and nature's elements in enlightening ways. To experiment with selflessness as a critical practice, and ethnography as an ethic – instead of an academic method.

This meant further applying the principles of critical thinking, distancing, and a body and soul immersion to the experience I was living, for a better understanding of the social mechanisms at stake without having to, somehow, instrumentalize this knowledge for my publication record and academic credits.

* * *

My narrative begins with ethnography as an ethic. It unveils emotions like feeling weird, insecure, and trying to find one's way out of emotional confusion by constantly leaving one's comfort zone – not as an escape, but as a confrontation. It embraces doing, and experimenting along the way, to better understand what critical practice can be in the name of, without losing sight of self-distancing. It opens ways to reclaim one's body and relationship with the elements following years of emotional and physical trauma.

Ethnography is, more than a method, the ground to build a reclaimed narrative – of the self, of otherness, and of the surrounding world. It can use different forms of storytelling to better reach out to various levels of perception and understanding: writing (either scholarly, poetic, or the more intimate journal note), but also the visual language of still and moving images, and even drawings. Hybridizing different forms of storytelling incarnates the simultaneous multiplicity that people living in a form of liminality, in-between worlds, can experience. When these forms of building a narrative coexist, they also unveil new sensory territories and alternative apprehensions of knowledge. This plural narrative becomes a fluid, a sensorial scape, a comforting yet hazardous milieu rhythmed by the flow, where mutations and adaptations follow one another in aqueous plasticity.

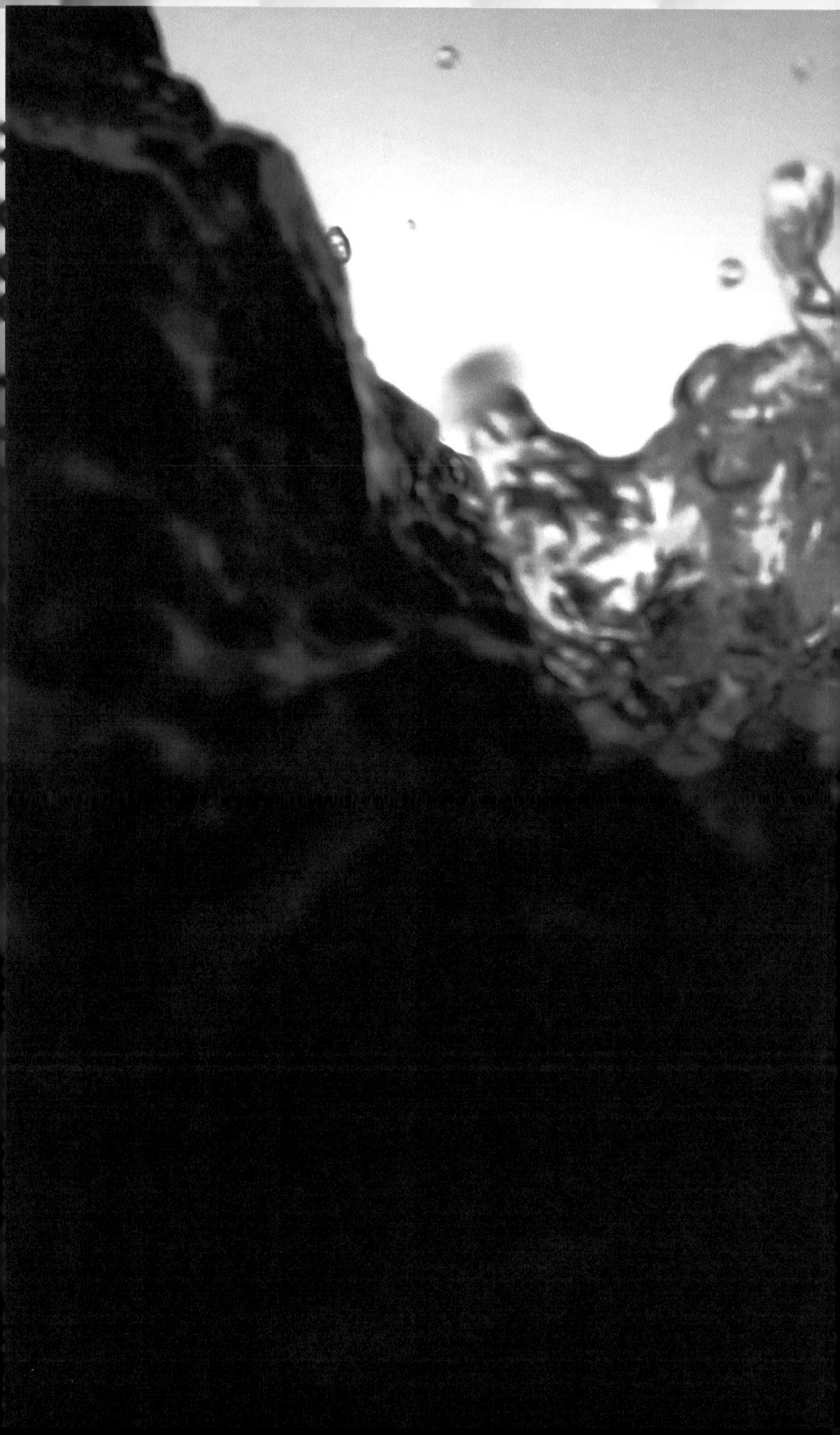

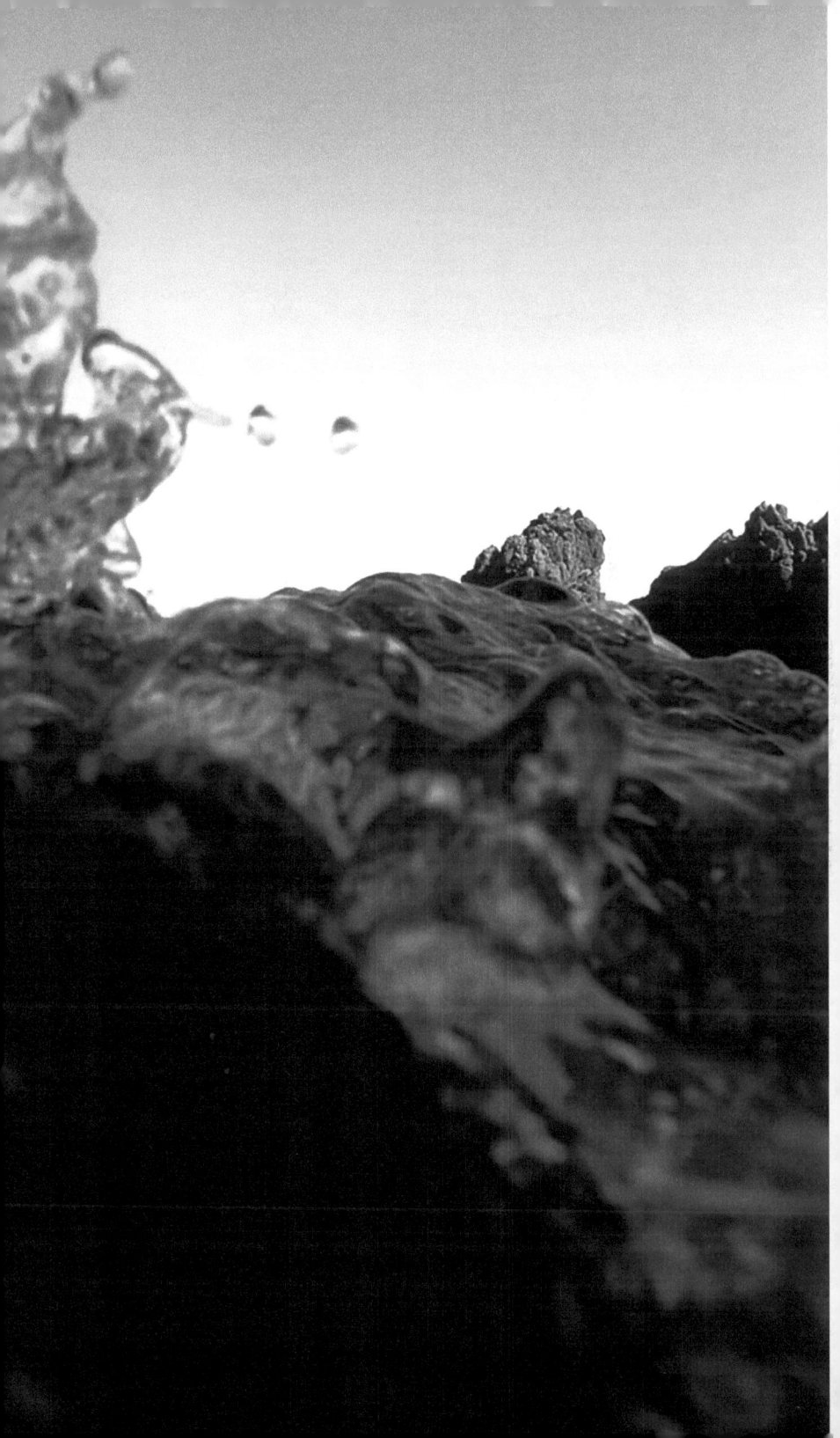

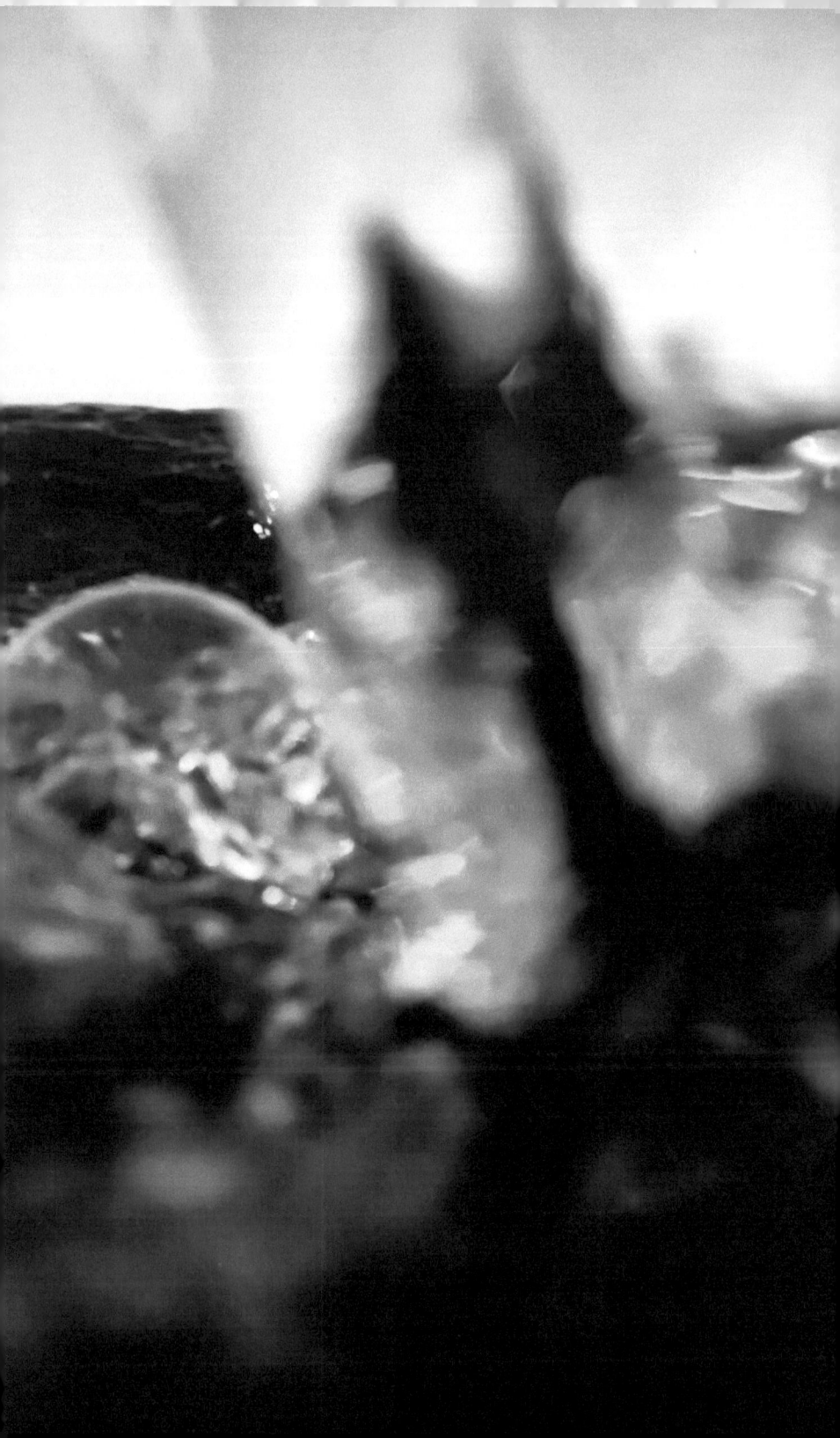

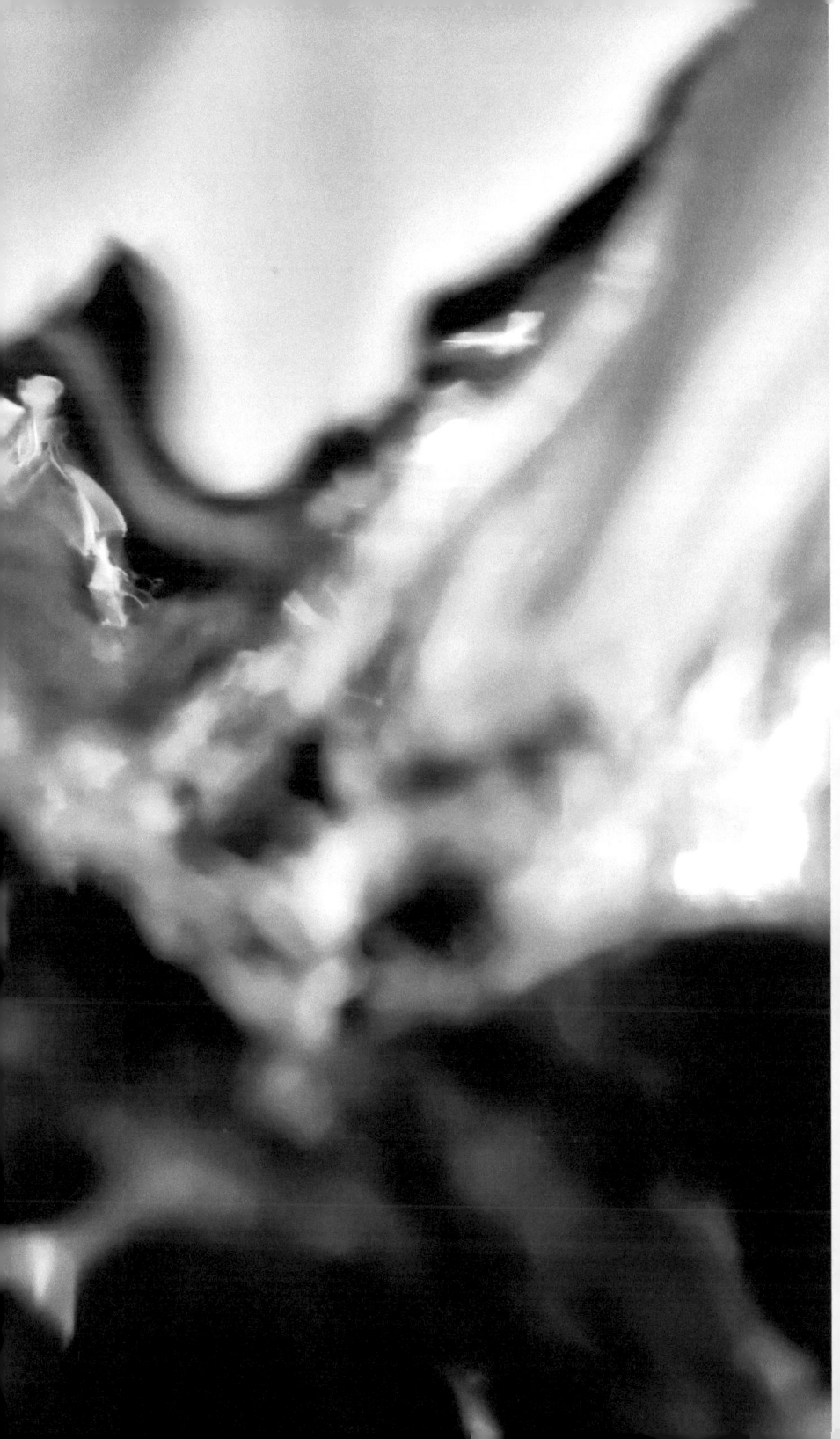

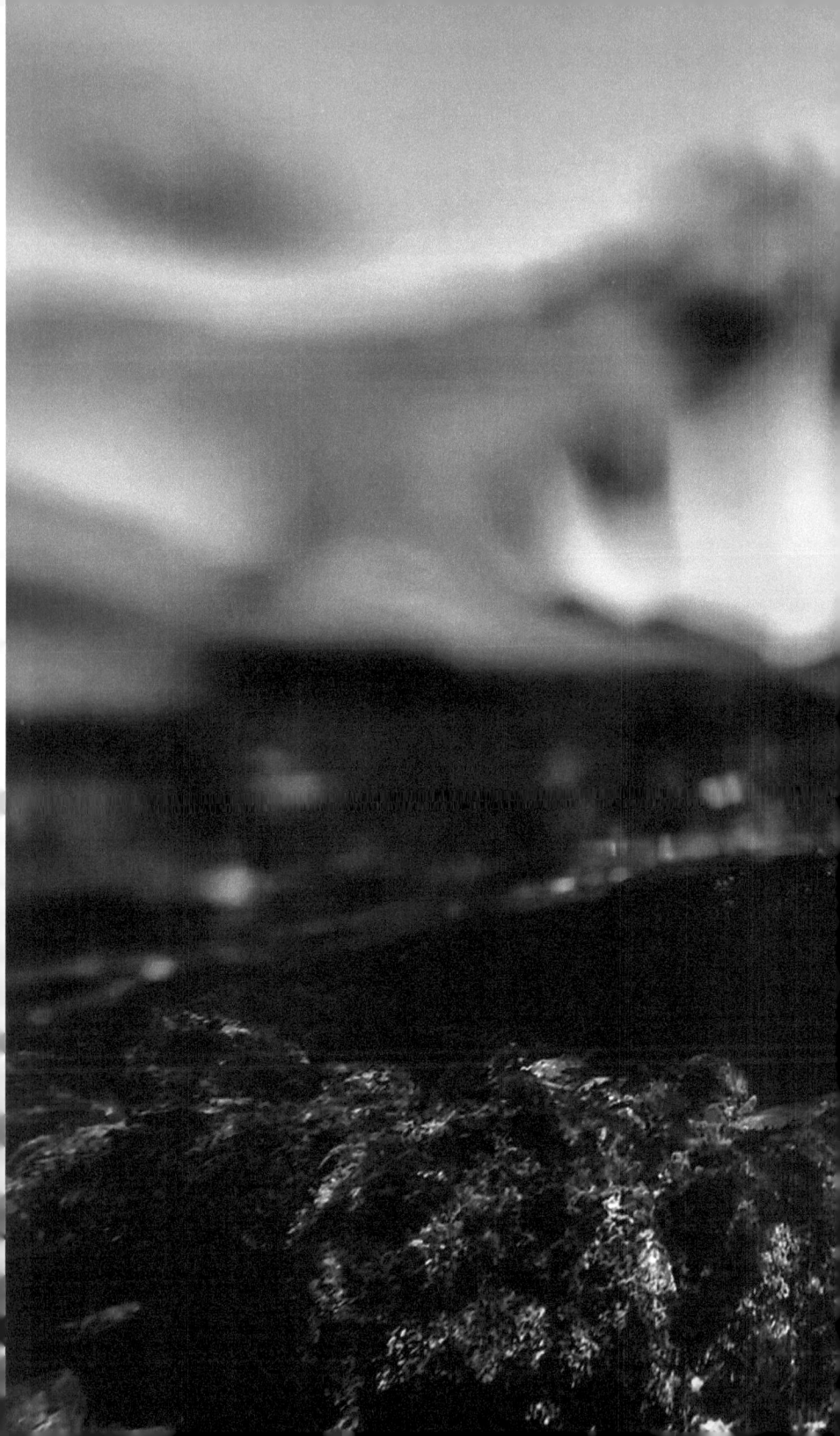

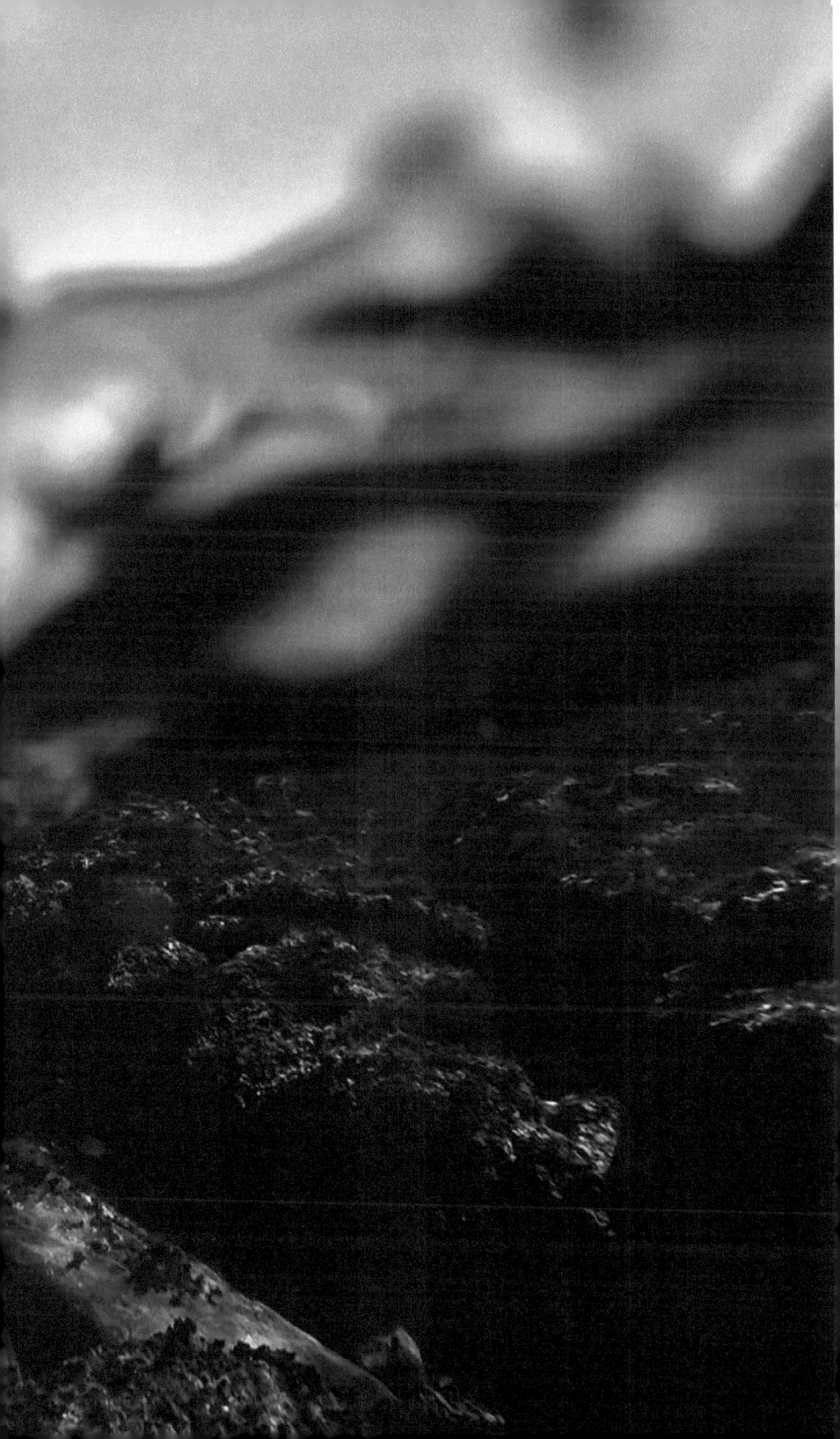

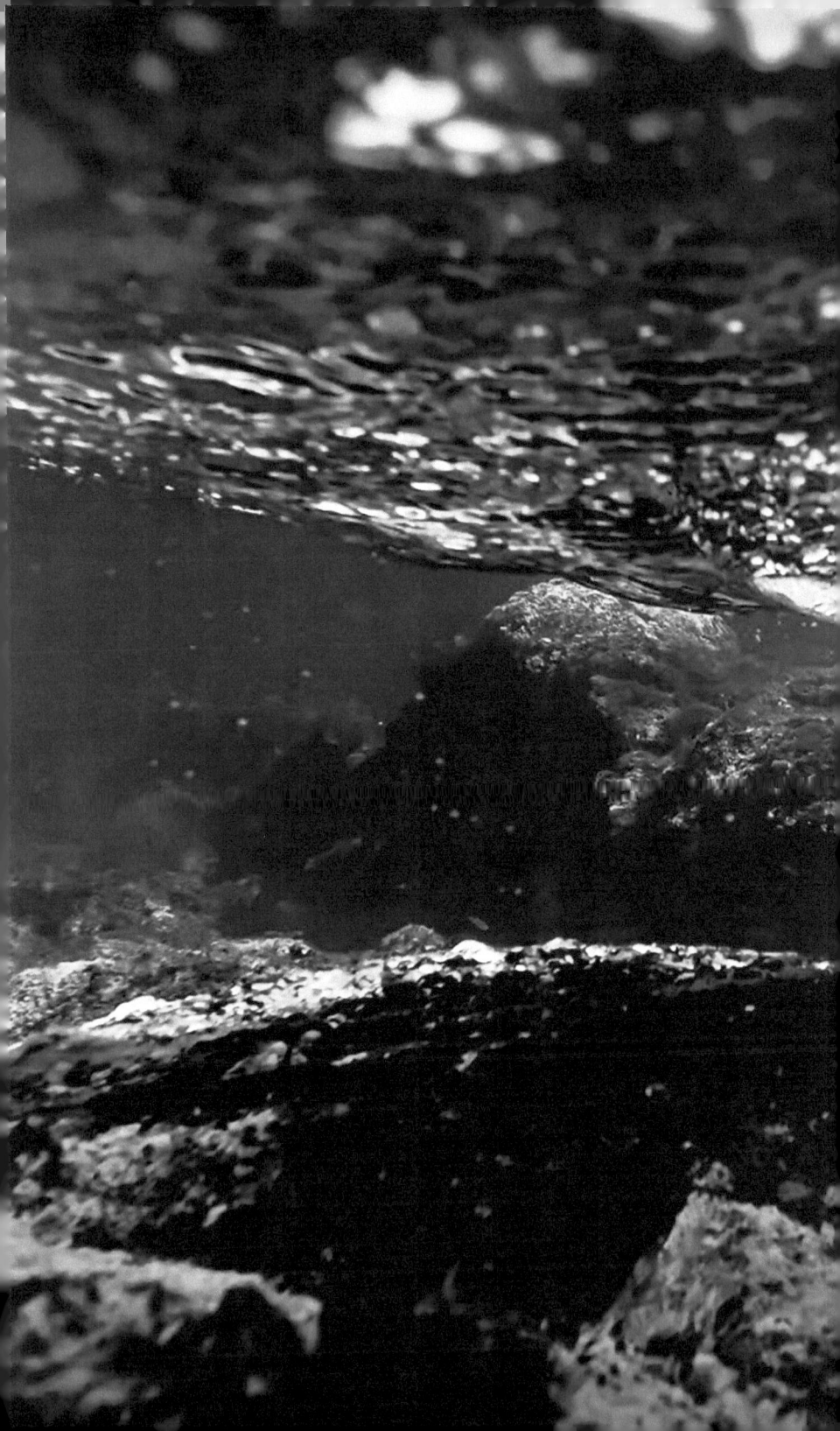

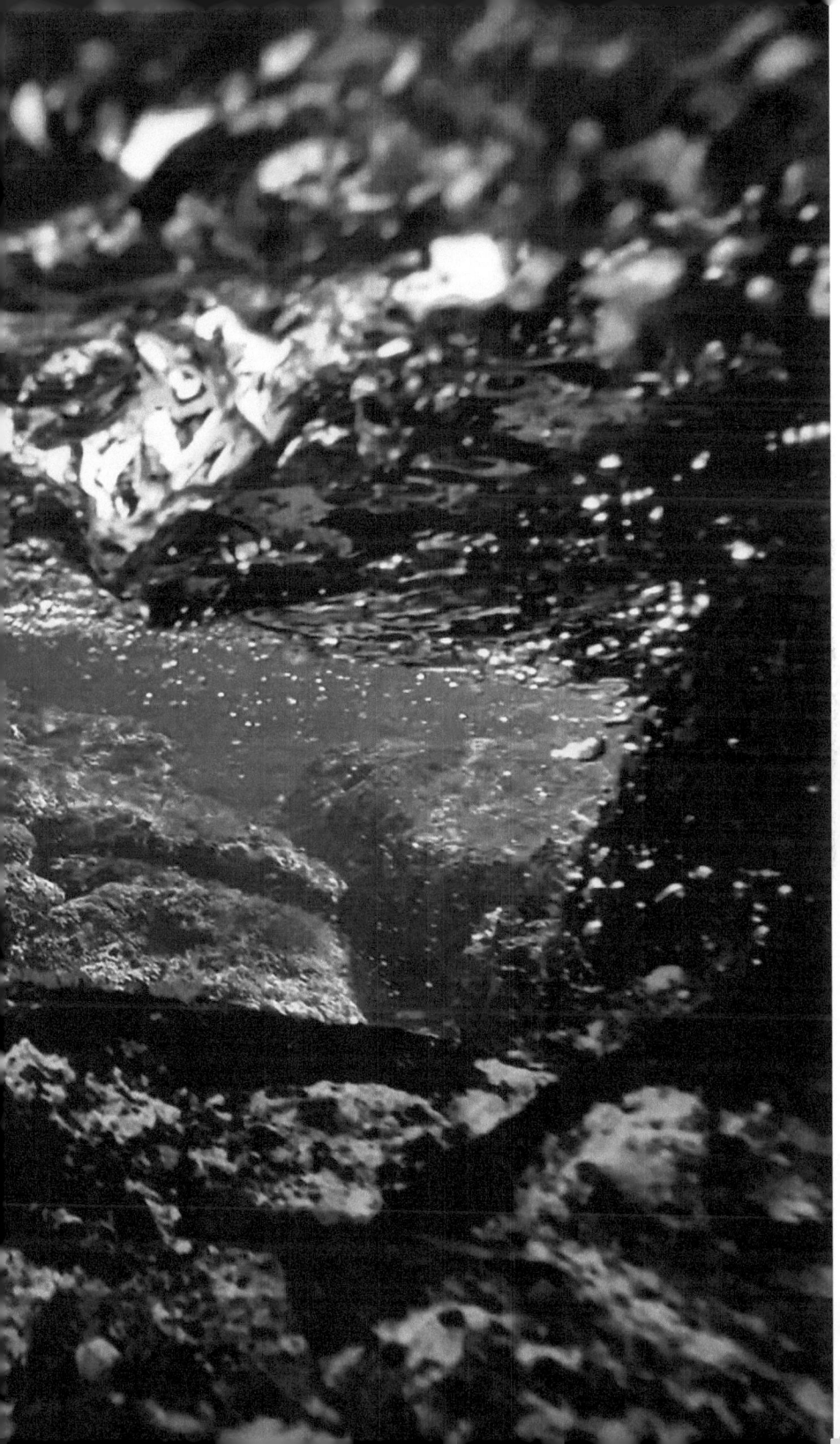

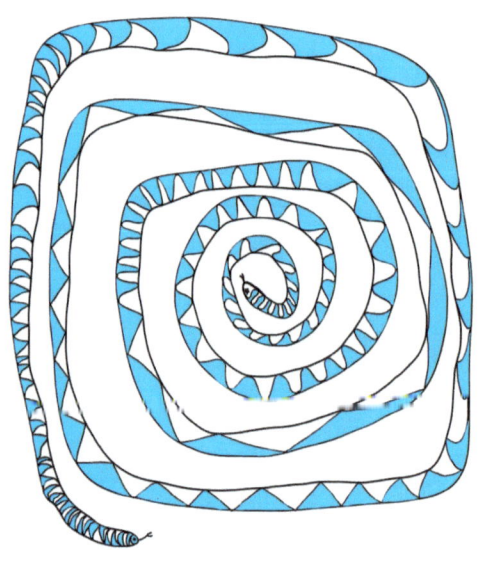

CHAPTER 2: FLOWING BODIES

How could we prepare for the lives we evolved into.
immersed in a substance we could not breathe,
and nevertheless called to be graceful.[1]

- Alexis Pauline Gumbs

Astrida Neimanis, an important figure in Feminist phenomenology, developed the notion of hydrofeminism. Hydrofeminism invites one to develop a consciousness of our bodies as bodies of water. The notion leads us to consider our bodies as aqueous entities, as opposed to the conception of ourselves as isolated individuals distinct from others and nature, inherited from Western rationality and its apprehension of metaphysics. This is the "organic, hierarchical dualisms ordering discourse 'in the West'" against which Donna Haraway's Cyborg is conceived.[2]

Our singularity turns itself into a fluid, constant and energizing circulation, bearing traces of our past just as the premise of our future. Our human bodies become connected to, the result of, and flow into, a hydrological cycle from rain to ocean to marine snow on seafloors – and back again. Bodies of water epitomize the paradox of evolving in a dense, multiple world: unique yet plural, here and now, yet then and there, stationary yet steadily moving. Bodies of water challenge the comfort of stable definitions and fantasies of unalterable realities. "Understanding our own human bodies as bodies of water (…) insists that we relinquish any lingering

---

1. Gumbs, Alexis Pauline (2022). *Undrowned: Black Feminist Lessons from Marine Mammals*. AK Press.

2. Haraway, Donna (1987). A "Manifesto for Cyborgs: Science, Technology and Socialist Feminism in the 1980s." *Australian Feminist Studies* 2(4): 1-42, p. 16.

illusion of nature as separate from culture, or of humans as separate from the world around us."[3]

* * *

A core notion in ethnography – the most central notion for me – is embodiment: interiorizing norms, categories, knowledge, know-how and techniques from the population studied in the field. I dedicated most of my academic publications, field journal pages, and intimate reflections, to this notion and to what it entails. Embodiment is what made me pursue university degrees in anthropology and sociology, and what fed my fascination for ethnography among all other methods of investigation.

Bodies of water summon a different take on embodiment. They are an incantation of new forms of defining, experiencing, and making sense of this notion. From concept, embodiment becomes an ethos wherein the human nature of bodies is transcended and the distinction with the elements is blurred. From this blur, unclear and possibly uncomfortable connection, "a different ethic of relation and care between humans and the planetary waters that are increasingly in crisis" emerges.[4]

Aqueous bodies allow this improved understanding of the damaged nature of our home planet precisely because they constitute a transcendence of the solely human nature of our existence. Being more than human means not being separated from the water. Not being separated from water means that we should respect it and care for it as something intrinsically bonded to our own physical body.

* * *

---

3. Neimanis, Astrida (2021). "Bodies of water (we are all at sea)," *Rivus: A Glossary of Water*, edited by José Roca and Juan Fransisco Salazar, 23rd Biennale of Sydney, p. 76-77.

4. Ibid., p. 77.

If hydrofeminism is a poetic narration of male exploitation over bodies – and nature in general – inspired by the fluid and complex form of life that is water, it is also a metaphor for the ethnographer's embodiment into increasingly blurring and shadowy scapes. By embracing the field through long-duration immersion, the question I never stopped being obsessed with is: "Am I becoming someone else?" Especially because I was experiencing difficult conditions during my fieldwork, including sexual assault and moral harassment from colleagues and informants, immersing myself in the field helped me reclaim my mind and body, while having the healing feeling to disincarnate from this very same body and become someone else. Becoming a body in water, having to learn again how to use it with the fluid's own conditions and rules, is at the same time limiting and empowering – demanding and cathartic. It is about doing with the water, and not against: adapting, finding harmony with how the fluid operates on what you thought was your corporality.

Most divers I know reason in terms of controlling the water and conquering its physics, while considering the water as a danger to overcome by sheer force. Like somebody else's body to control.

Breathe.
Control your breath.
Follow your lungs: up, down, steady.

Don't resist.
Slowly, aware of your extremities.
Trust.

Stop breathing, hold it.

Flowing bodies have fluid voices. These voices are "cracks on the dominant and oppressive narratives [and] open up spaces for new stories to be told."[5]

---

5. Latent Community (2021). "Hydrovisions." In "Dam" in *Rivus: A Glossary of Water*, edited by José Roca and Juan Fransisco Salazar, 23rd Biennale of Sydney: 118-125. p. 122.

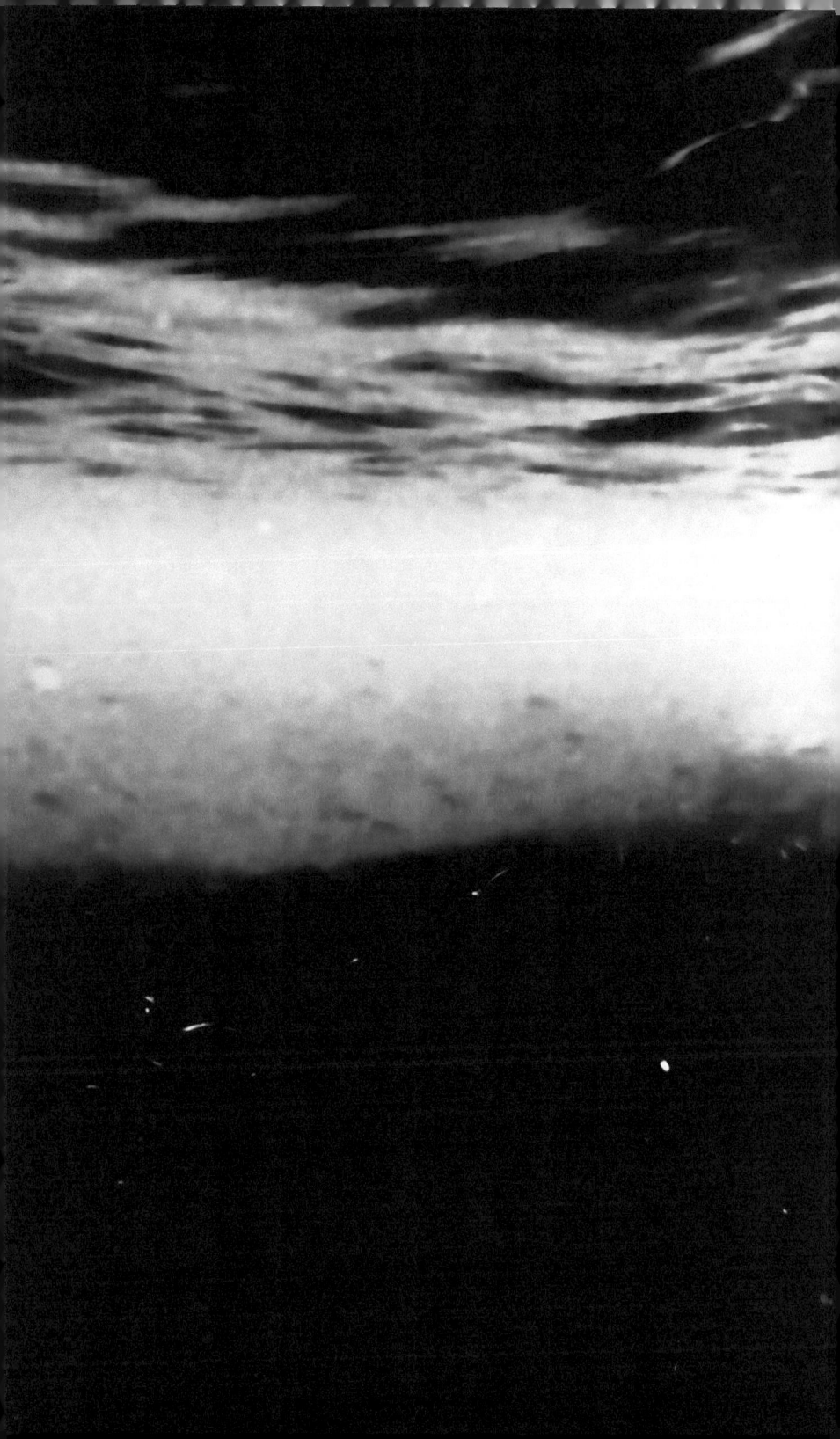

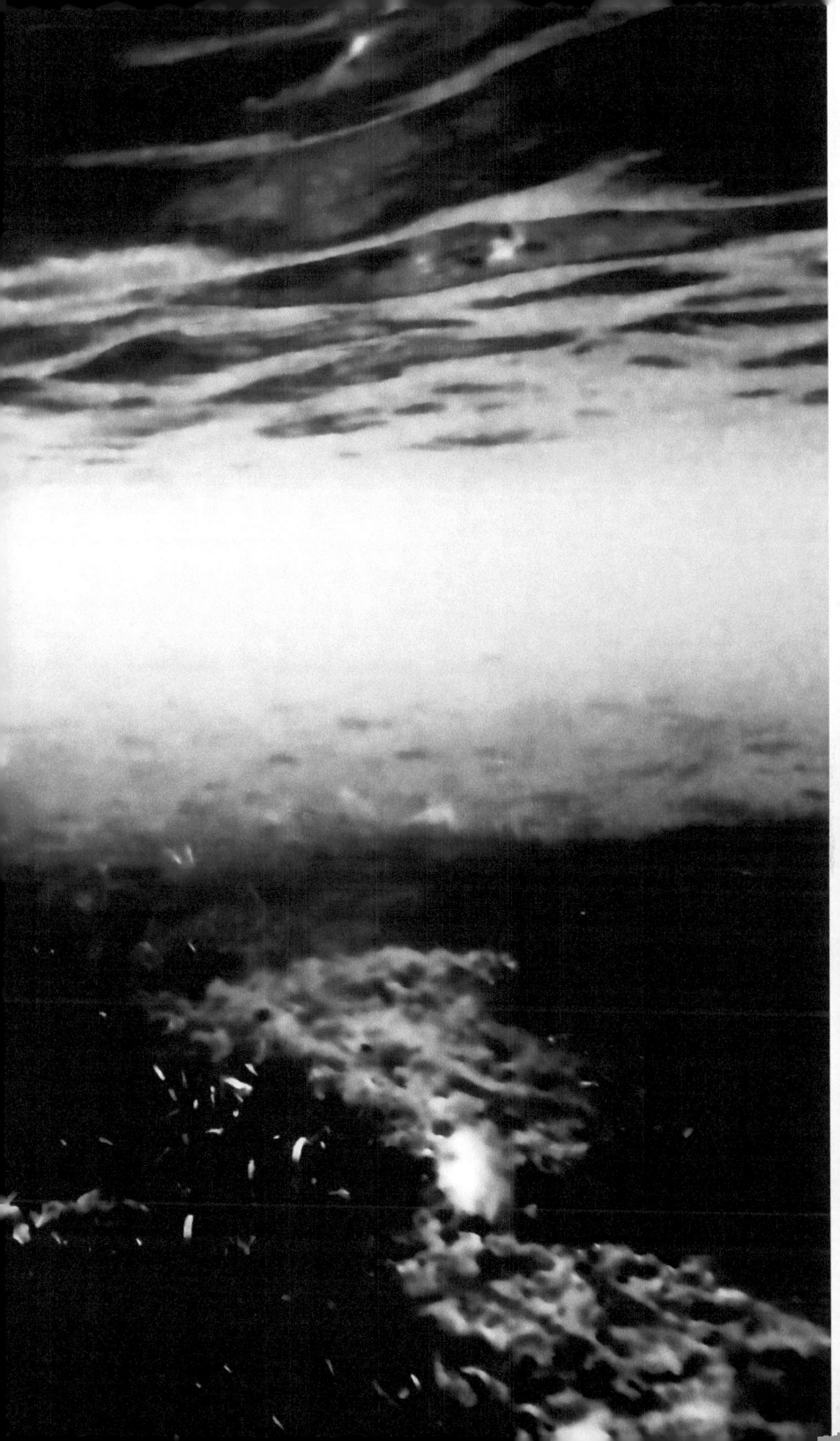

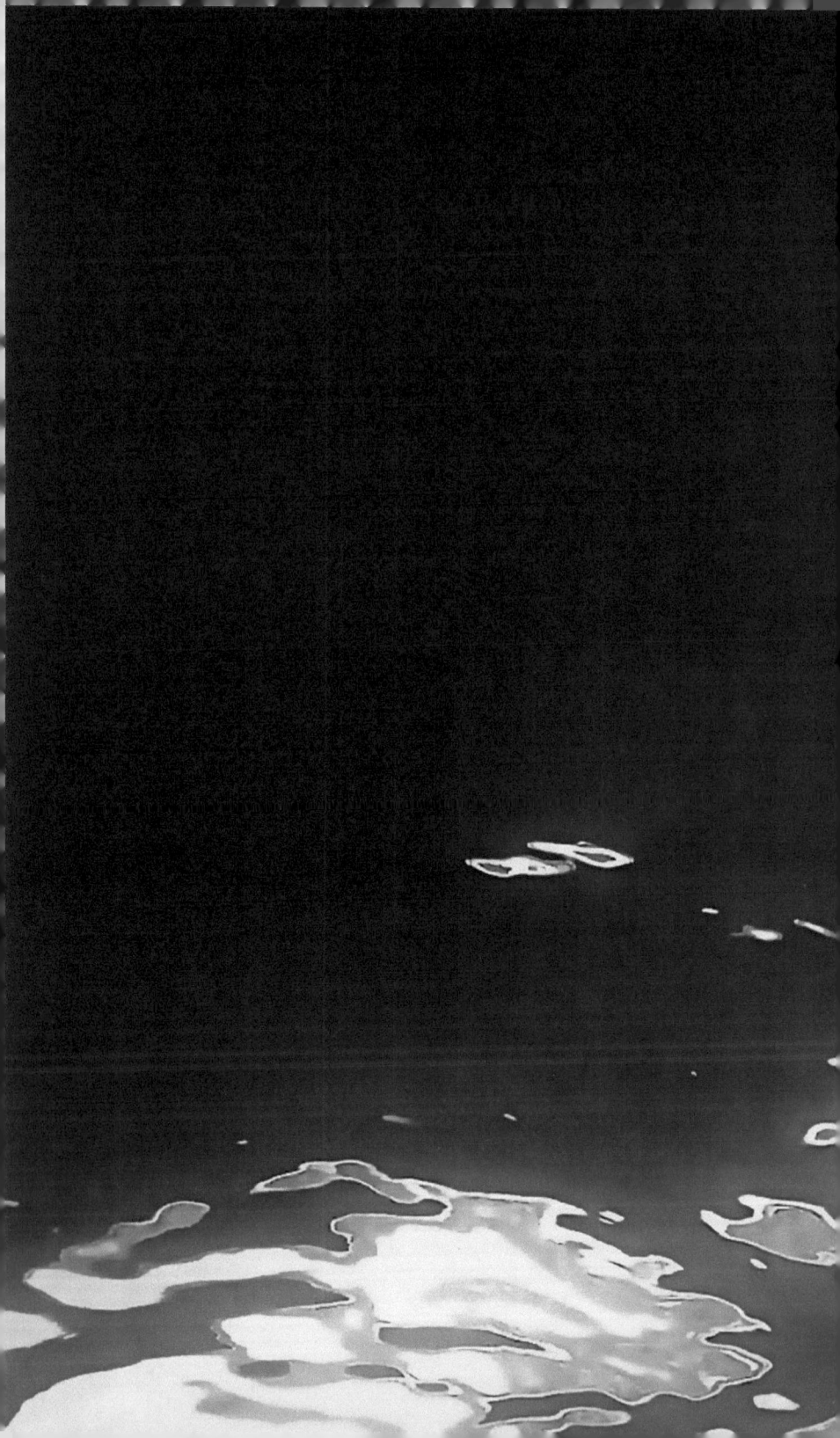

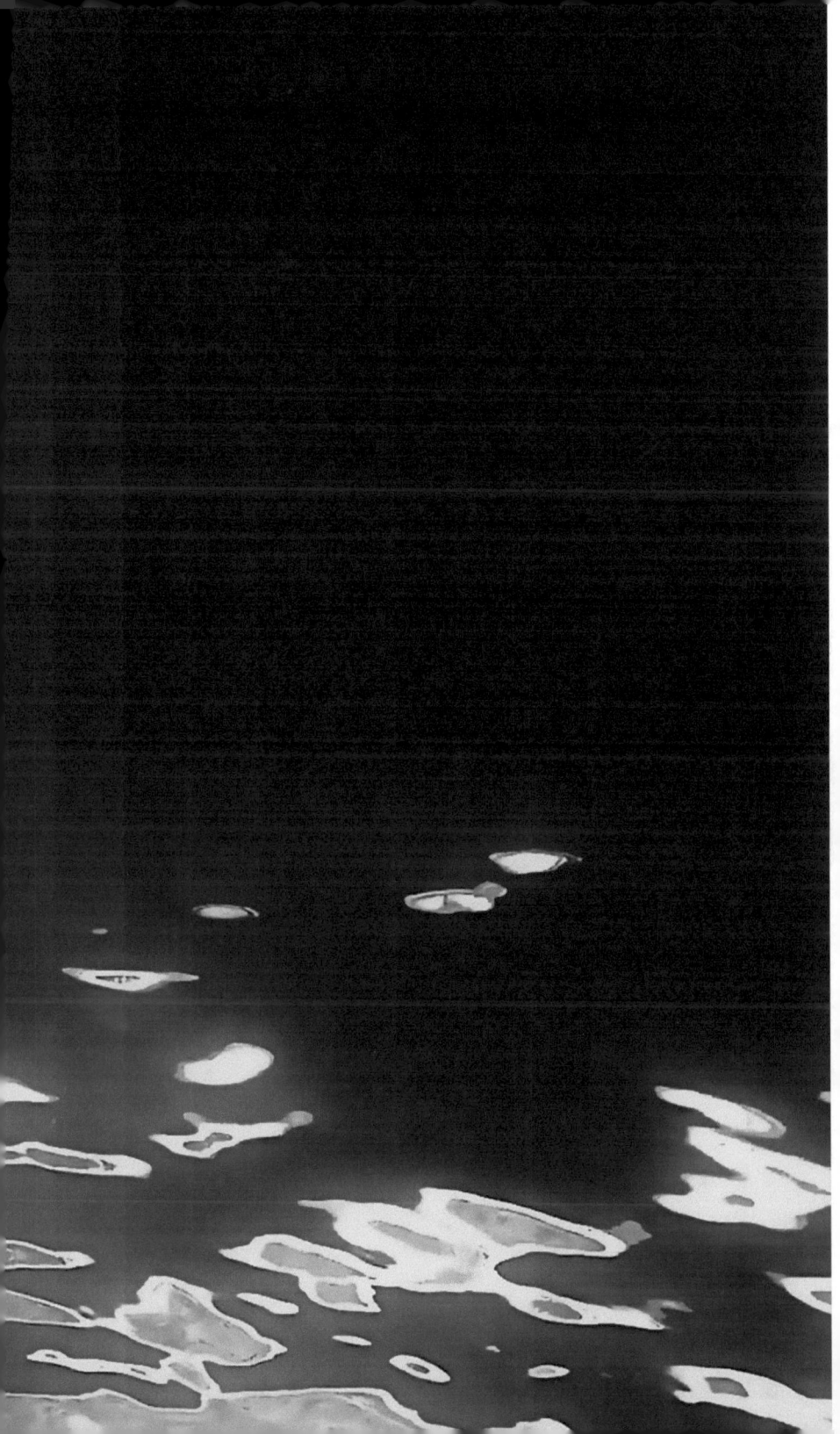

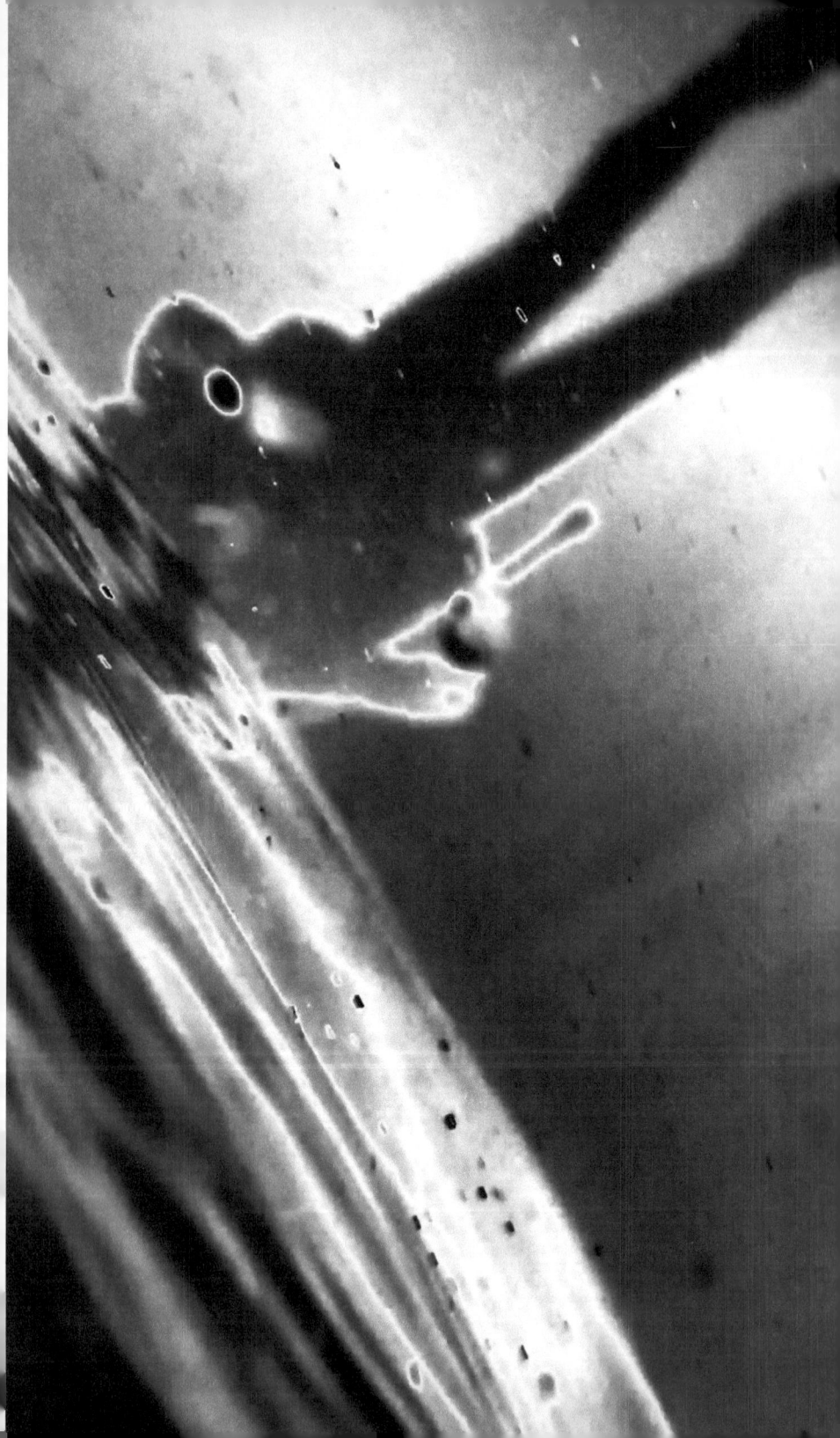

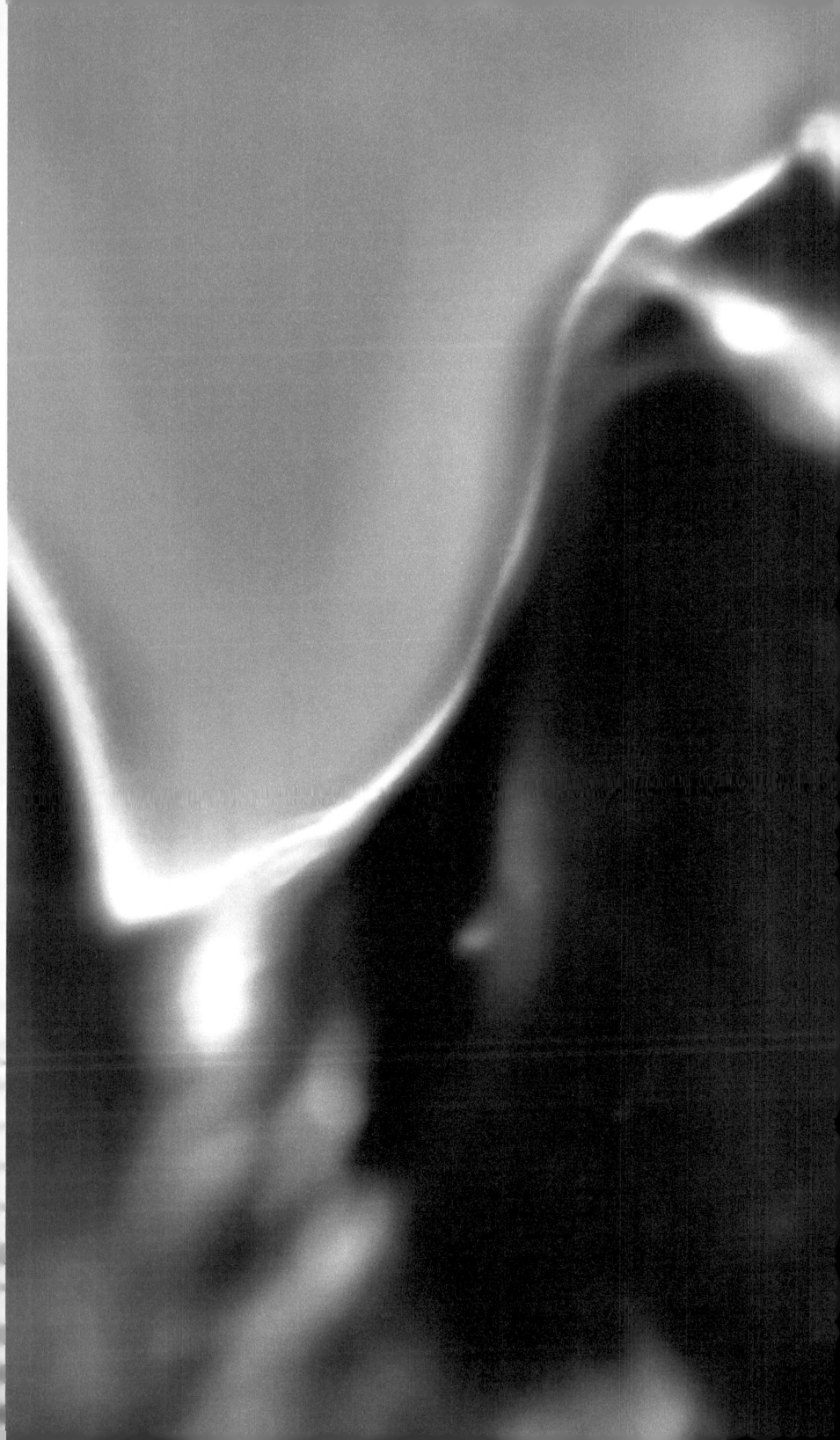

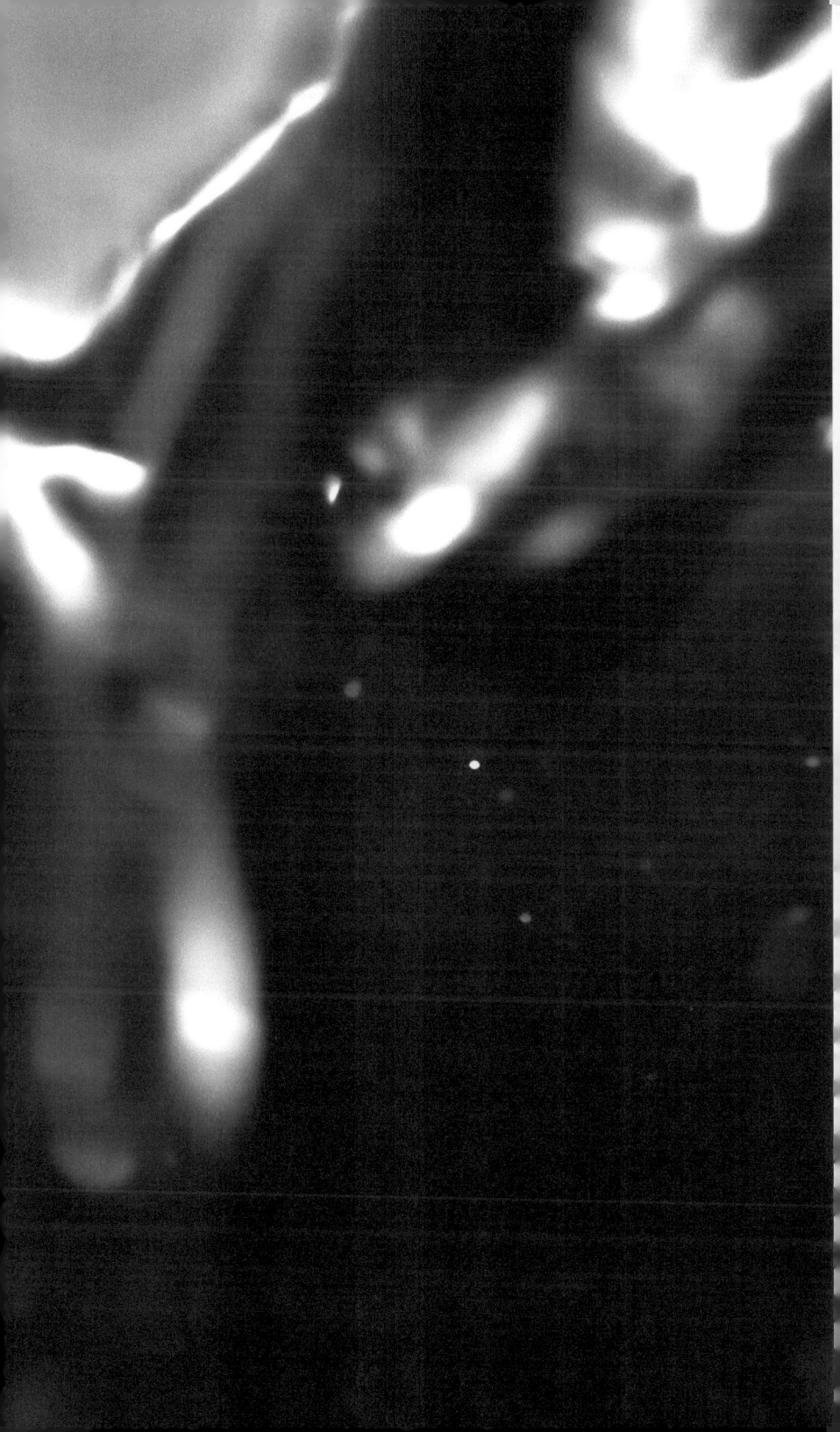

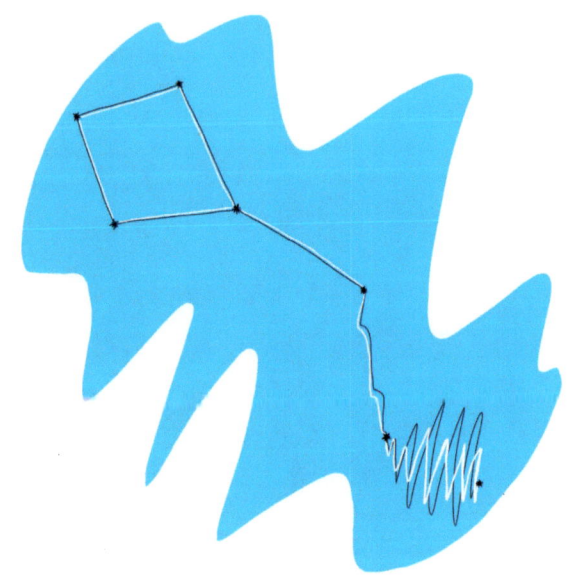

CHAPTER 3: MYTHOLOGIES

No objects, spaces, or bodies are sacred in themselves.[1]

- Donna Haraway

During my commercial diver training, many of my classmates were actively engaged in intense muscle-building training. This meant they were getting up at 05:00 in the morning to go to the gym. They were carefully measuring quantities and selecting their food (in addition to mass gainer food supplements). Because all our lunches were taken collectively on the site where we were spending the day (a military training base for amphibian combat, i.e., a lake partly owned by the diving school equipped with underwater training sites, etc.), these meal breaks were group ceremonials honoring androgenic strength – that very same that was used to hold the hydraulic drill or the pneumatic water lance.

[June 2022]

A commercial diver is not supposed to ask questions about the whys, he's just supposed to do what he's being told to do (and moreover a female diver) as a mindless executant. Hopefully, all instructors don't have the same ideal of what a good commercial diver is/will be. But I don't fit most of their models, as I'm regularly reminded (often despite what I actually do). It happens almost every day that how they perceive my actions and assess my competencies contradicts how I actually work – they see a distorted version of my actions.

---

1. Haraway, Donna (1987). A "Manifesto for Cyborgs: Science, Technology and Socialist Feminism in the 1980s." *Australian Feminist Studies* 2(4): 1-42, p. 16.

Sexism is omnipresent in masculinized professions like commercial diving – or astronauteering (outer-space travel). Such professions are inherited from a social history where women were either absent or invisible, leading to their difficult inclusion (and recognition) in contemporary times, and to biased representations affecting the assessment of their abilities. These biases entail ruptures asking to be fixed.

While these professions are largely framed by body-machine entanglements (wet bell, umbilicals, helmet...), gendered representations relate to the set of technologies and artifacts developed for, and used by, professionals. A Russian cosmonaut once told journalists their only female colleague was "bad at spacewalks" because she was "too small for her suit." Russian suits are not tailor-made, but manufactured in standardized sizes fitted to a specific male body whose size and weight are selection criteria in cosmonaut recruitment campaigns.

As an in-training commercial diver, I had similar experiences using standardized suits and instruments conceived for male bodies. I once dove with a helmet constantly filling up with water because the sealing neoprene neck was too large – which led me to order a made-to-measure one that nobody else could use during my training to prevent its distortion. I was used to doing underwater welding with latex gloves three times my hand size, which prevented me from feeling where the electrode and welding torch I was holding were on the piece of metal on which I was working. I dove with a constant-volume latex suit with weighted boots so large that my body floated up and down within the suit, and my feet constantly came out of the boots.

Where there is a standard, there is a dominant model to which the standard is fitted. When there is a dominant model, there is a plethora of alternatives. Invisibilization feeds the assumption of an inferiority to the dominant model – and their inadequacy to the standard.

* * *

These gendered biases bare traces of the exploitative and destructive relationship of men with nature, which is part of a broader system of power relationships. The production of a certain manhood and virility, associated with physical strength and carelessness, relates to the exercise of domination over nature through the alteration and destruction of the environment.

Ecofeminism lies in this articulation of gender dynamics and ecological damage. It bears the awareness of an intimate connection between domination over nature and domination over women, non-cisgender and non-white people because both these dominations are exercised as a result of a separation of nature from culture in Western rationality. This separation led white men to believe in a hierarchy of life forms they should head – and consequently, exploit to their will. This separation bears a long-time intellectual history of misconceptions of the underseas, of the cosmos, and of all the living forms in-between.

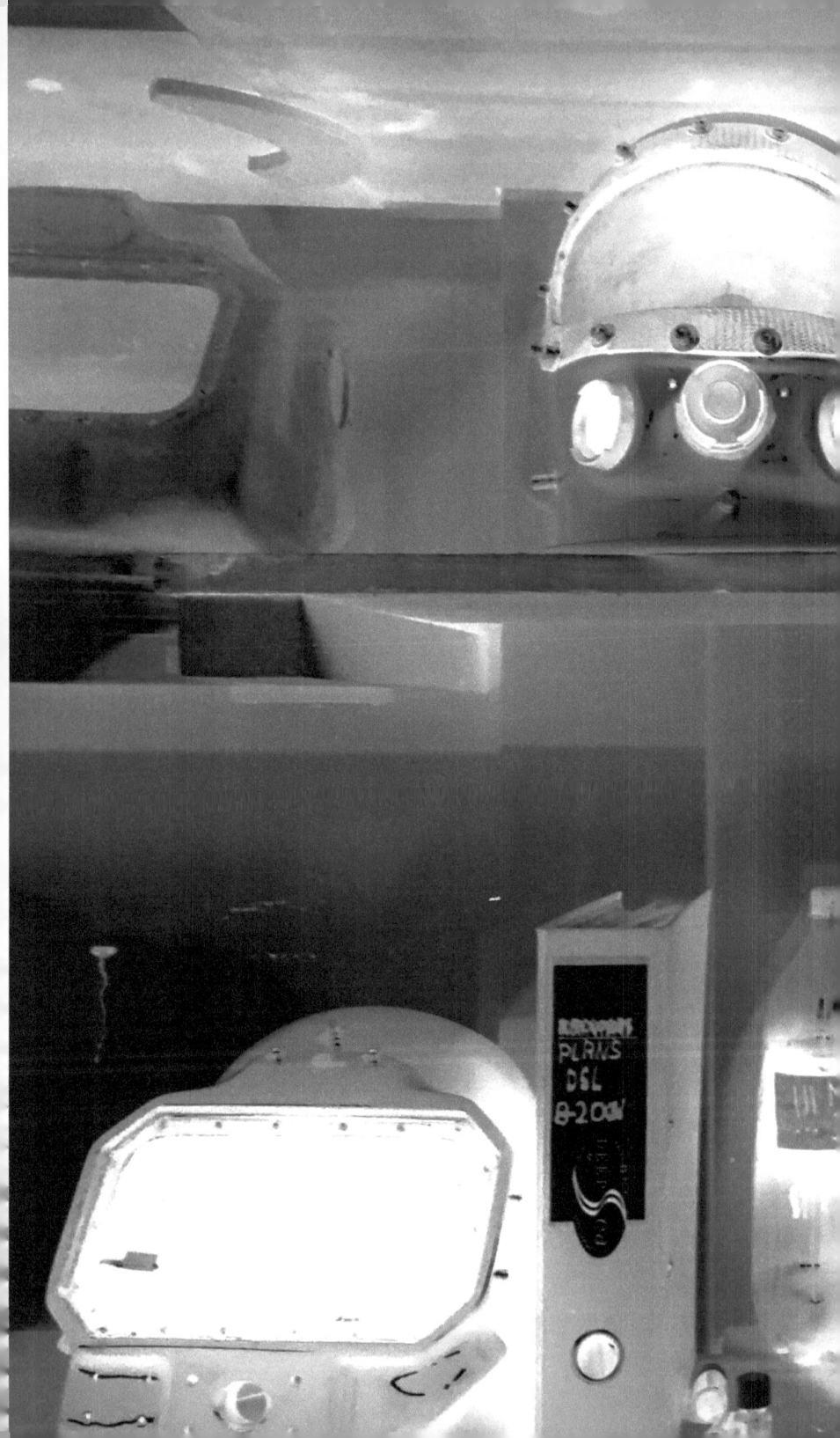

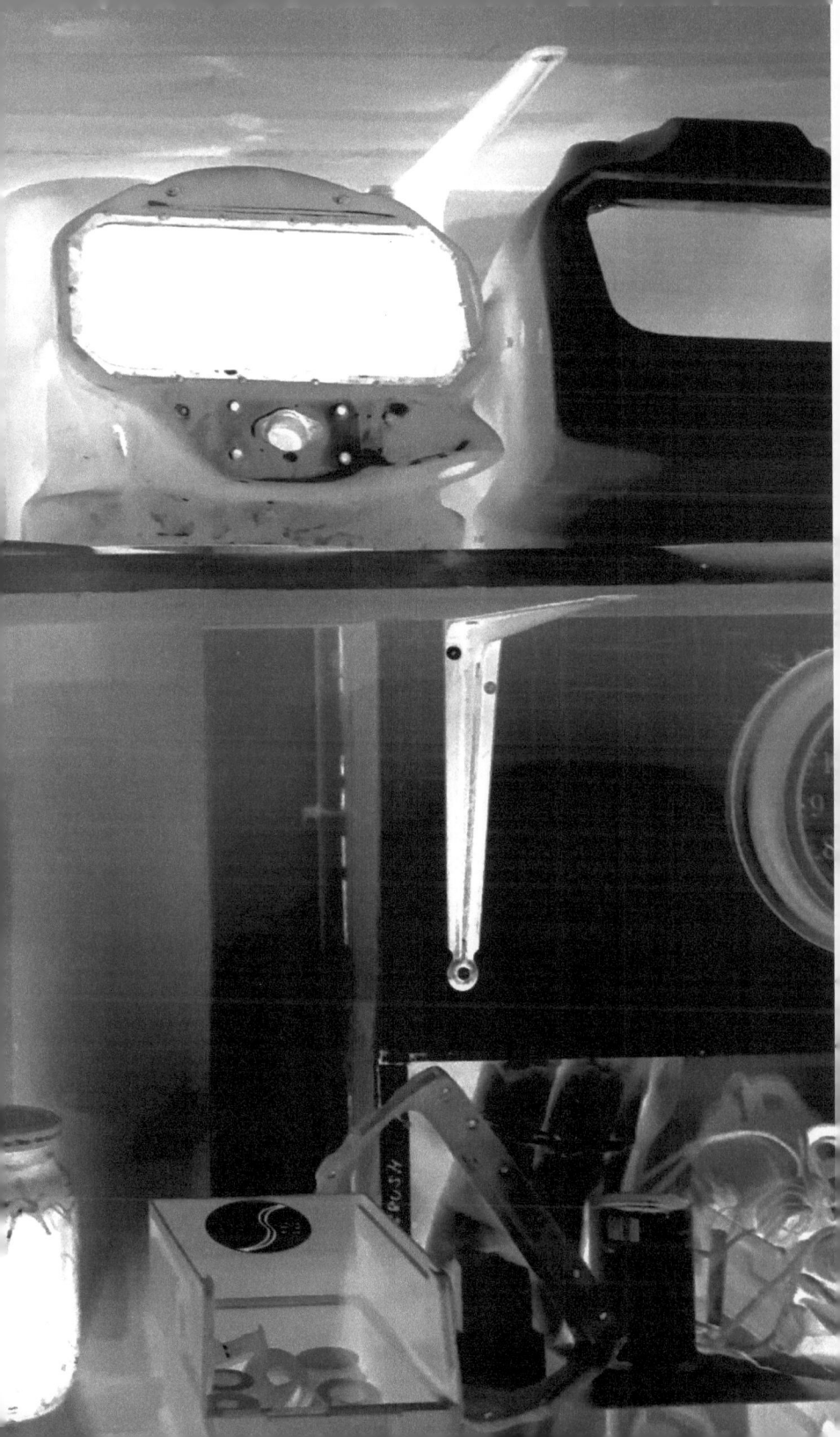

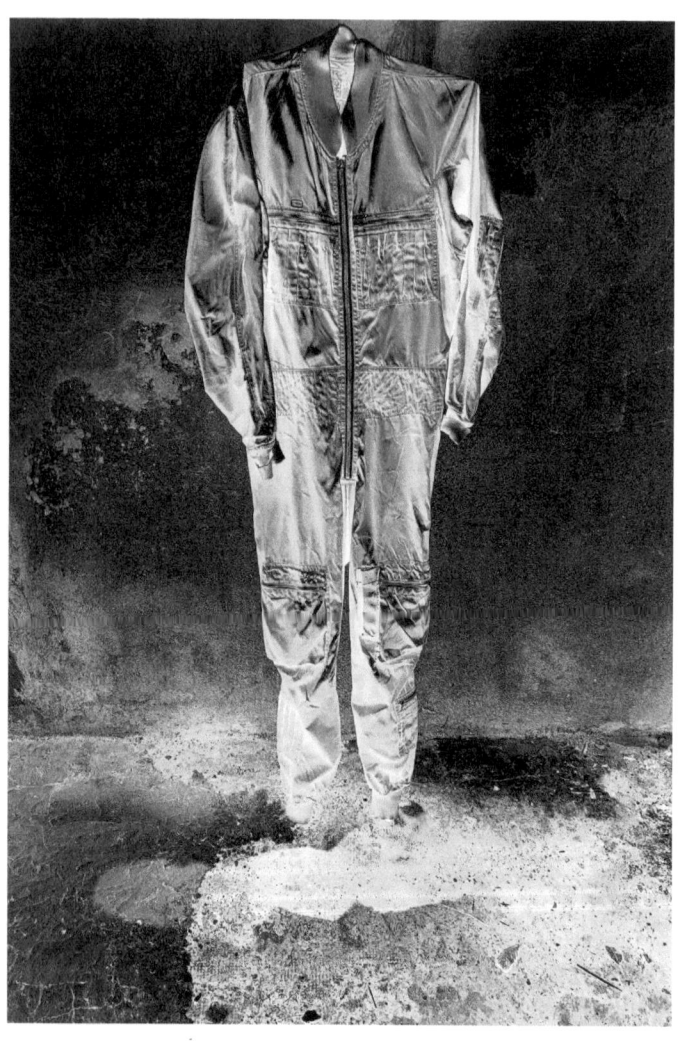

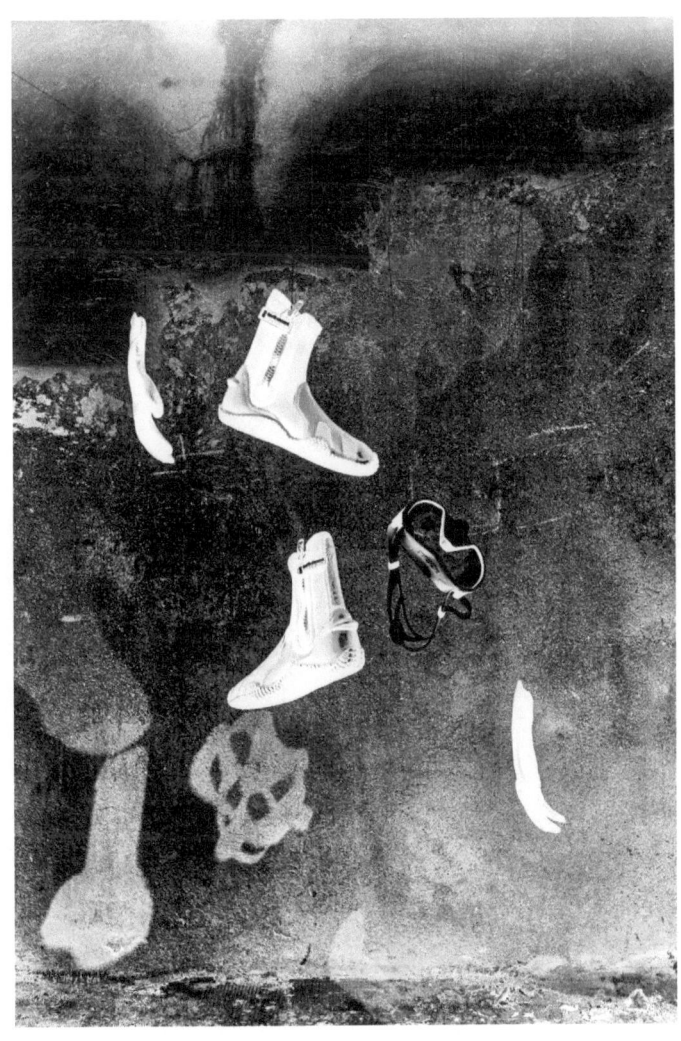

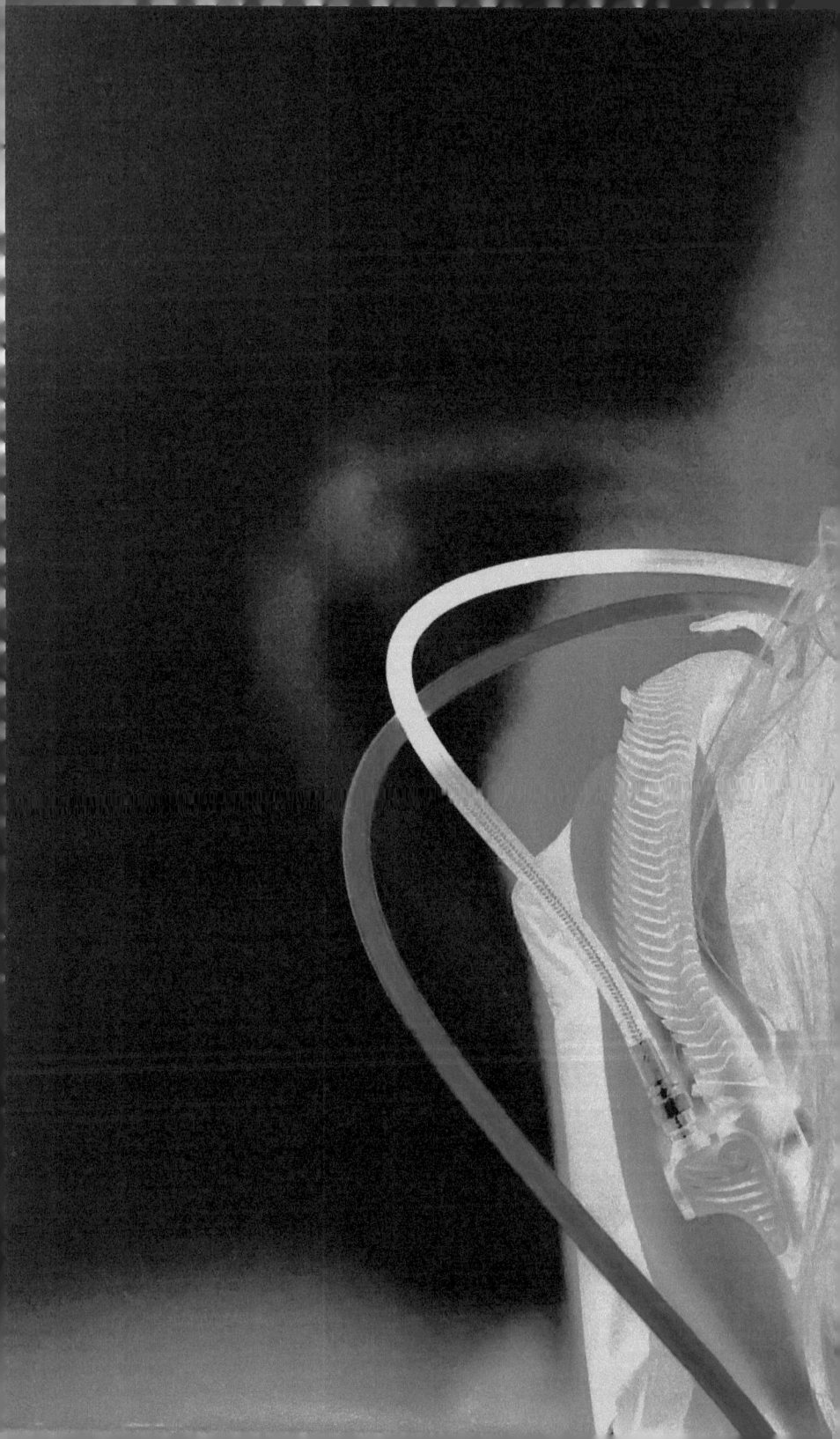

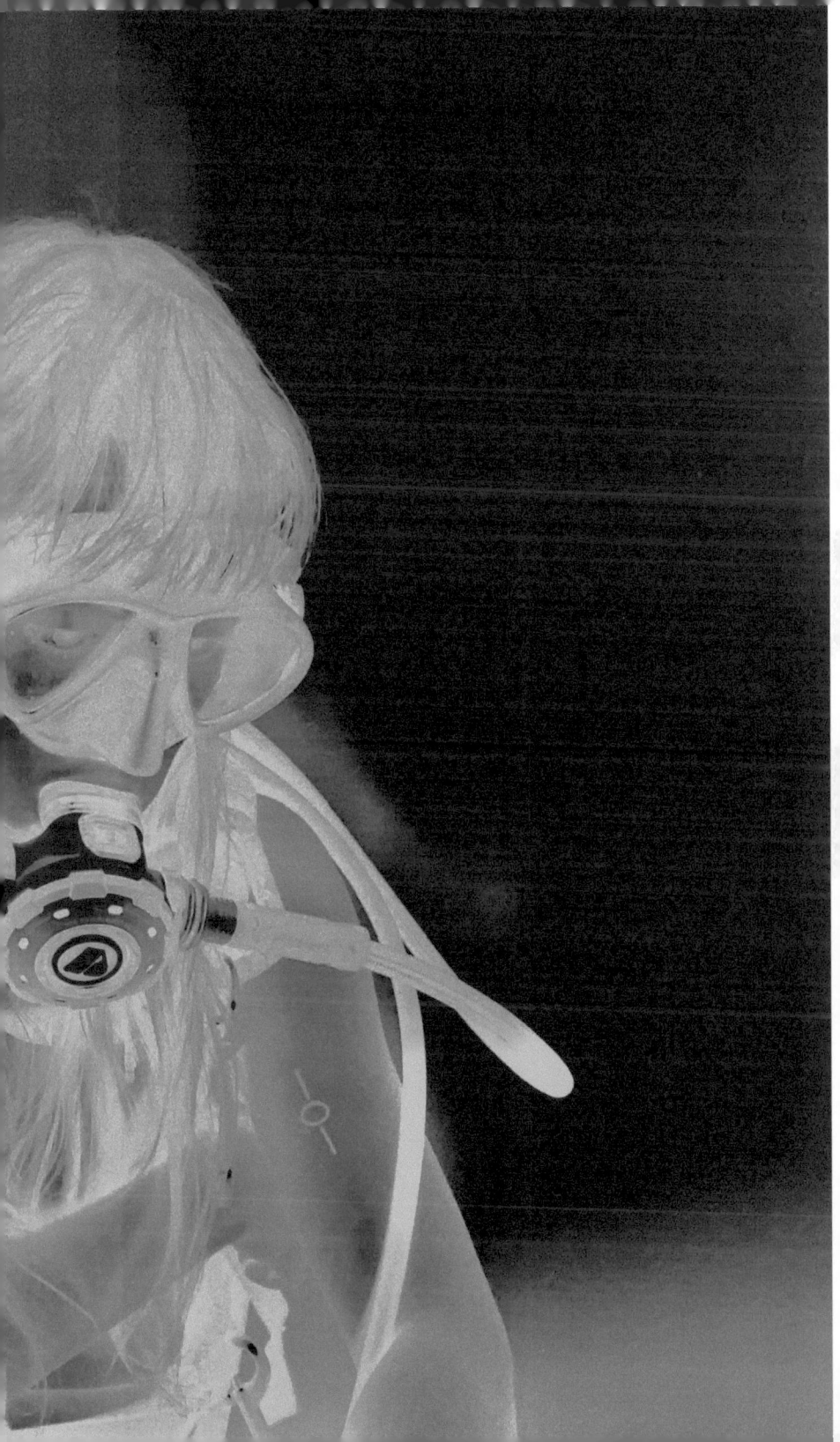

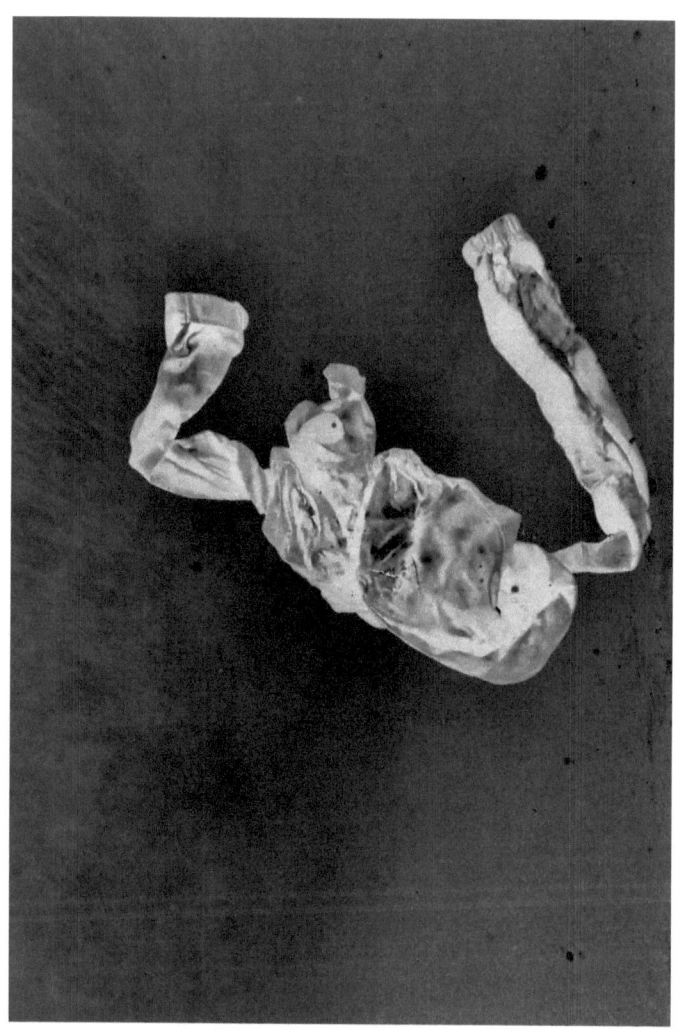

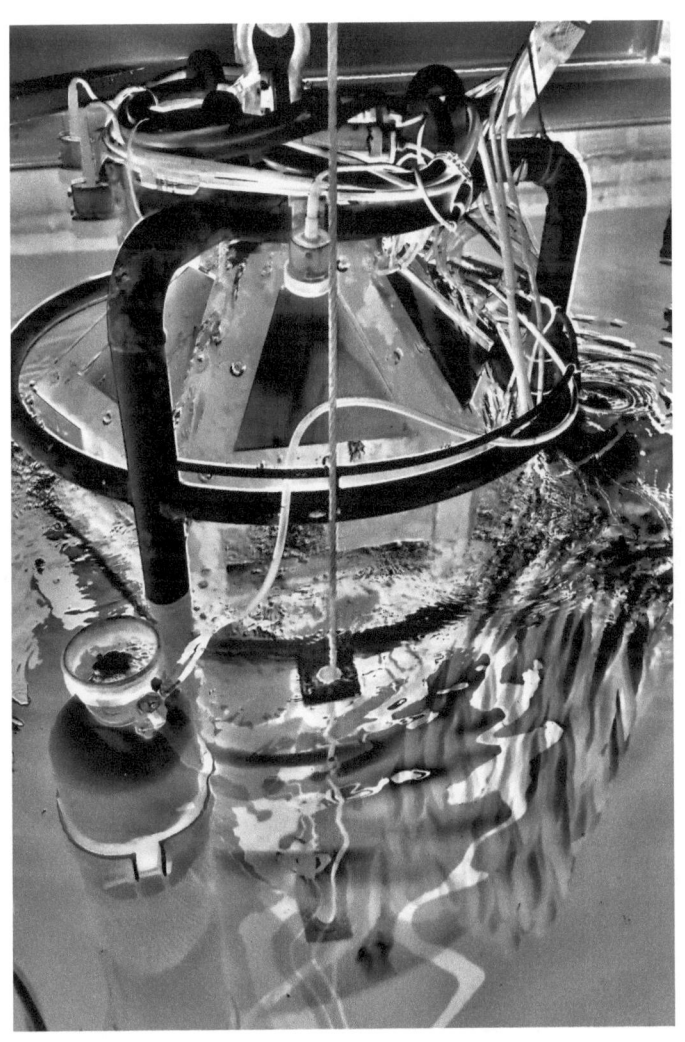

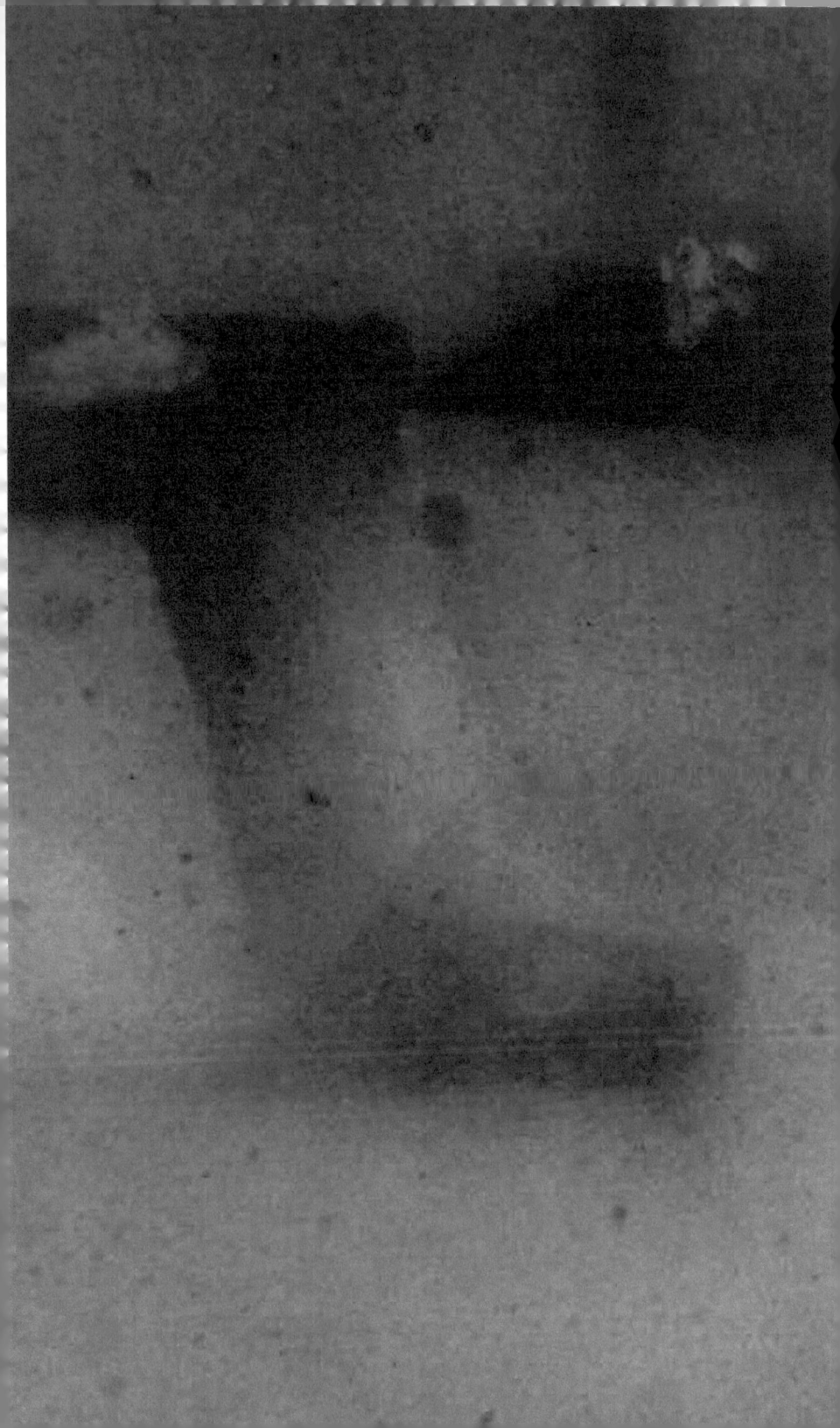

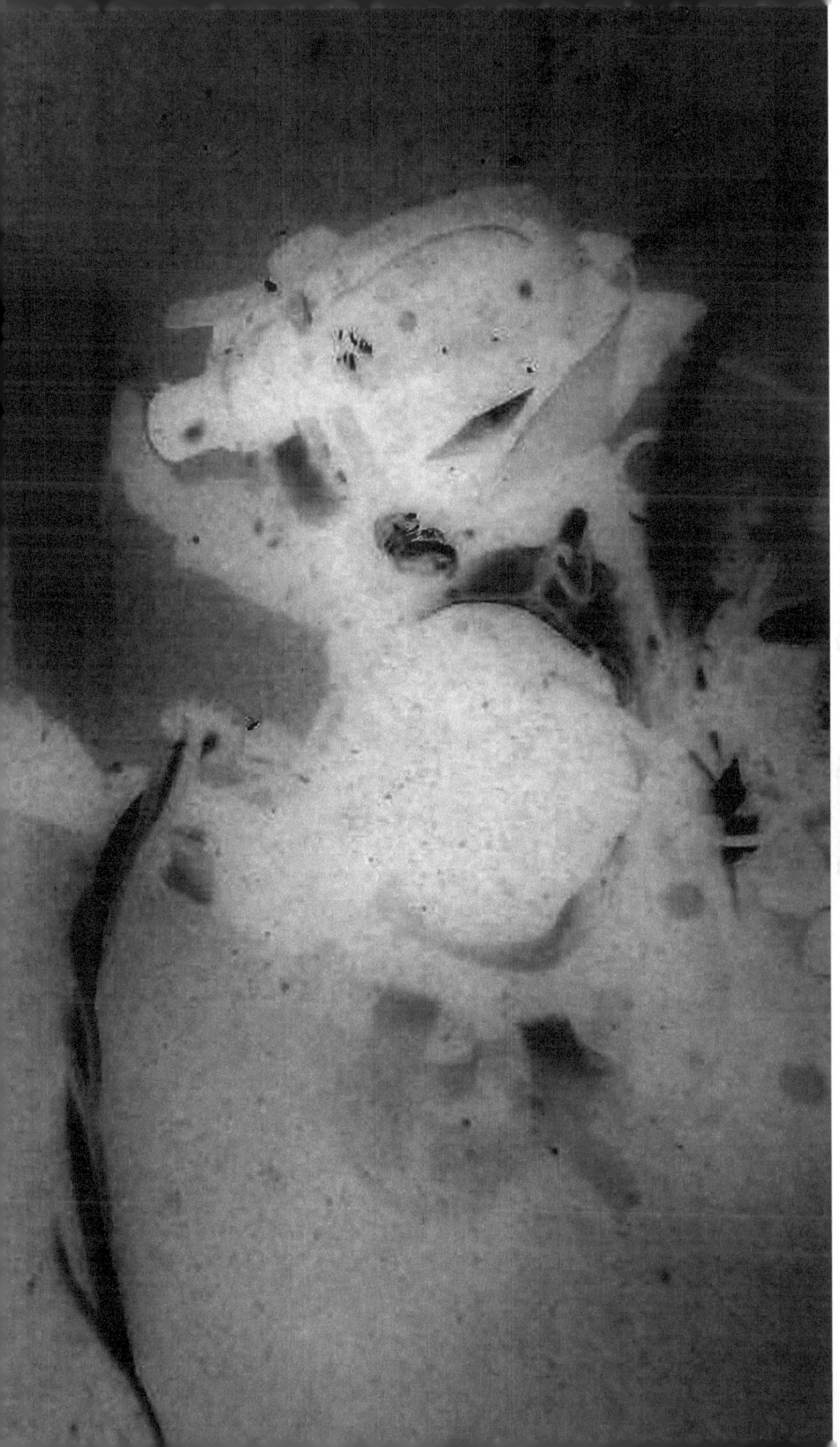

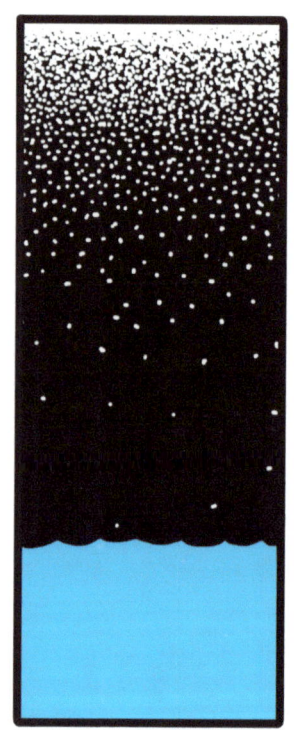

CHAPTER 4: COLONIAL SCAPES

Humanity is eternally condemned to suffer because of our delusion of separation.¹

- Kiki Smith

The lessons provided by hydrofeminism, and ecofeminism in general, are connected to those provided by holist cosmologies, against which Western rationality was developed. According to holist systems of beliefs, human beings are not separated, nor independent, from the natural and cosmic environment in which they live.

> Their destiny is connected to the stars.
>
> Their daily life is rhythmed by the elements and their celebration.
>
> Their family circle includes celestial bodies and other entities inhabited by spirits in the natural world.

For Zuni Native Americans, the Moon is not only a living body but also a sacred entity due respect and ritual performance. According to this cosmology, sending a rocket and landing on the Moon to drill its ground and take samples back to the Earth is a dangerous, inconsiderate act likely to bring disorder in the global harmony of the cosmos (of which human beings are an active part).² Similarly, Indigenous ecologies present water as a sacred body carrying life, time, memories, dreams, premonitions – all those being signs of divine communication with the mortals.

---

1. Smith, Kiki (2022). "Puddle", in *Rivus: A Glossary of Water*, op. cit., p. 376.

2. Young, Jane (1987). "Pity the Indians of Outer Space: Native American Views on the Space Program", *Western Folklore*, 46 (4), p. 269-279.

Either in the form of

```
r       i       v       e       r    s           ,
d       e       l       t       a    s           ,
e   s   t   u   a   r   i   e       s            ,
p   u   d       d       l       e       s        ,
w       a       v       e       s                ,
w   e   t       l       a   n   d       s        ,
r   e   s   e   r   v   o   i   r       s        ,
o       c       e       a   n       s            ,
                        o                        r
r       a       i       n                        ,
```

water bears consciousness and the promises of cosmic connection.

Water remembers our ancestral associations, of our birth, of growth. Water as a ritual helps me make sense of the everyday, of the everyday rebirth, of sunrise and sunset.[3]

- Jason de Santolo

The apprehension of the underwater world that many divers have, as a hostile environment that human bodies need to master and tackle to survive, was sired by this cosmology opposing the suspicion of the world as a machine of perpetual motion, and its appreciation as a coherent living organism.

The underseas have been shaped, through worldwide history, by representations, fantasies, and colonial frameworks related to territoriality, otherness, and resource utilization as part of the very notion of exploration. A conception of exploration as a conquest over wildness for the benefit of industrialization, and as the expression of power by a human species un-

---

3. de Santolo, Jason (2019). "Sun Showers and White Ochre." *Sydney Review of Books: New Nature Essays*. https://sydneyreviewofbooks.com/essay/sun-showers-and-white-ochre/

conscious of its connection to the stars. Subaquatic experiences, including how these experiences are put into words and images, are historically situated and deeply culturally grounded.

The Enlightenment, this very same period of Western history where the rational spirit rose against spirituality, magic, and the sensible realm, conceived the Earth's oceans as a source of misguiding and obscure intrigues, preventing the search for not only knowledge, but truth.[4] Water was a concealing element impossible to overcome, and as a consequence, a hostile element acting as a shield against the intellect.

* * *

Early underwater aesthetics reflect the vision of the underseas both as a hostile space and as a territory to explore. Creative methods can serve as a strong counter-narrative to these aesthetics, and help craft a cosmic language of the underseas tethered to its ecology.

A language where visuals build a meditative and reflexive wandering in the depths of the Mediterranean sea, and an ode to Oddness.

A language where imagery investigates the eeriness of submarine weightlessness and bodies' resilience in undefined landscapes.

A language subverting underwater imagery techniques and their visual effects.

A language acting as an alternative to the exploitation of subaquatic wilderness and as a celebration of its enlightening shadows.

In oceanography and marine biology, the temperature of organisms is key

---

4. Roman, Hanna (2019). "The logic of the invisible: Perceiving the submarine world in French Enlightenment geography", in *The Aesthetics of the Undersea*, edited by Margaret Cohen and Killian Quigley, Routledge, p. 42.

data (although often understudied) in the analysis of their biochemical mechanisms. In the case of micro-algae, the temperature is a selection criterion in their sampling for their utilization as photobioreactors – which rely on the micro-organisms' photosynthesis and thermophilic capacity. Temperature is thus deeply related to the industrial cultivation of marine micro-organisms.

Thermal imagery techniques are usually used to document, measure, if not hunt underwater fauna by night or in low visibility conditions. As a consequence, the rare underwater uses of thermal or infrared cameras are for recreational fishing. As for their terrestrial uses, thermal cameras are inspection instruments. They are used to locate and identify construction issues, weaknesses of a structure, or leaks. Their use is for detecting a problem that will likely require repair or construction – something that needs to be fixed. I wanted to subvert these uses. Inspired by previous art thermal photography,[5] and especially because of the limited caption of infrared in water, I conceived underwater thermal imagery as a powerful storytelling method, running counter-current to the colonial and industrial politics of the seas.

Underwater thermal photography, or thermography, builds an alternate narrative where life and exploitation are not only articulated around the heat of living things, but around how water actually rejects the imagery technique. As a living and sacred entity, water dismisses technologies conceived to identify man-induced failures asking for repair. The only distinguishable shapes remain at the surface (a tree, a hill), while the more it approaches water and is immersed, the less the imagery technique can capture anything else than the resilient heat of waves crashing on the shore and against the lens. Once fully submerged, the underwater life finally goes back to being an inscrutable enigma contesting rational knowledge.

While industrial culture for productivity relates to a progressive mass destruction of species and alteration of natural landscapes, unless if con-

---

5. I am particularly referring to the interdisciplinary artist, SMITH, represented by the Parisian Gallery Christophe Gaillard: https://galeriegaillard.com/artists/10773-smith/overview/.

sciously managed, thermal imagery tells of the selfless vitality and vibrance of these organisms (and of the fluid they evolve in), through their very invisibility. Through the deployment of a creative knowledge method, thermography allows a poetic wandering into underwater depths, connecting failed observation techniques with ecological resilience.

Creative knowledge methodologies revive connections, narratives, and practices supporting world ecologies. They open up ways of trying to retrieve and restore ancestral bonds that were once lost (un)intentionally. They unveil a desire to leave an imposed exile from the cosmos.

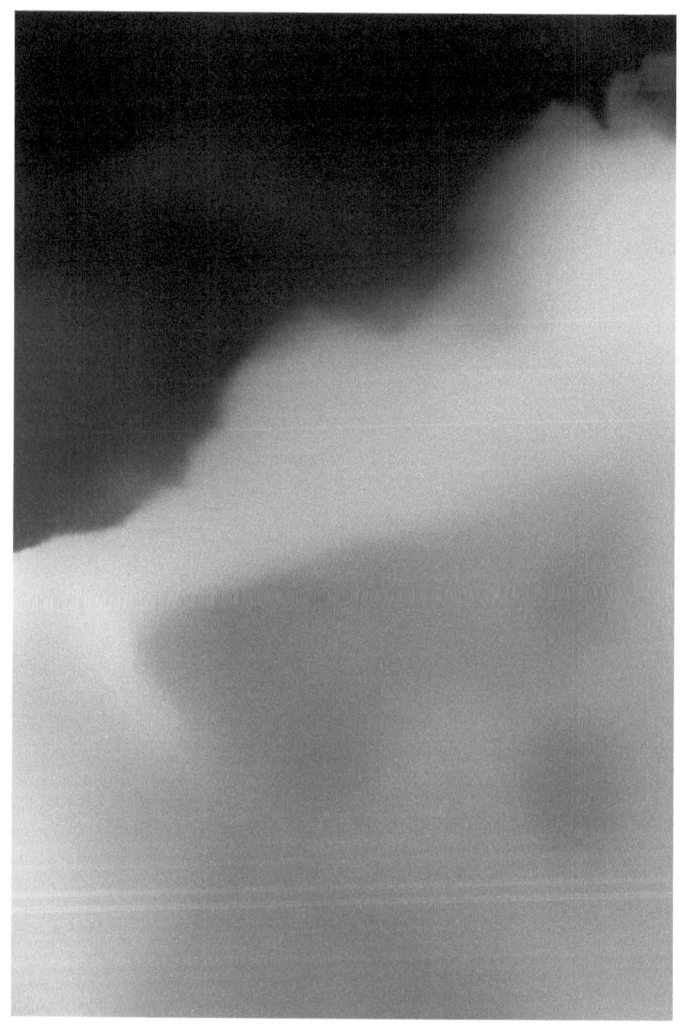

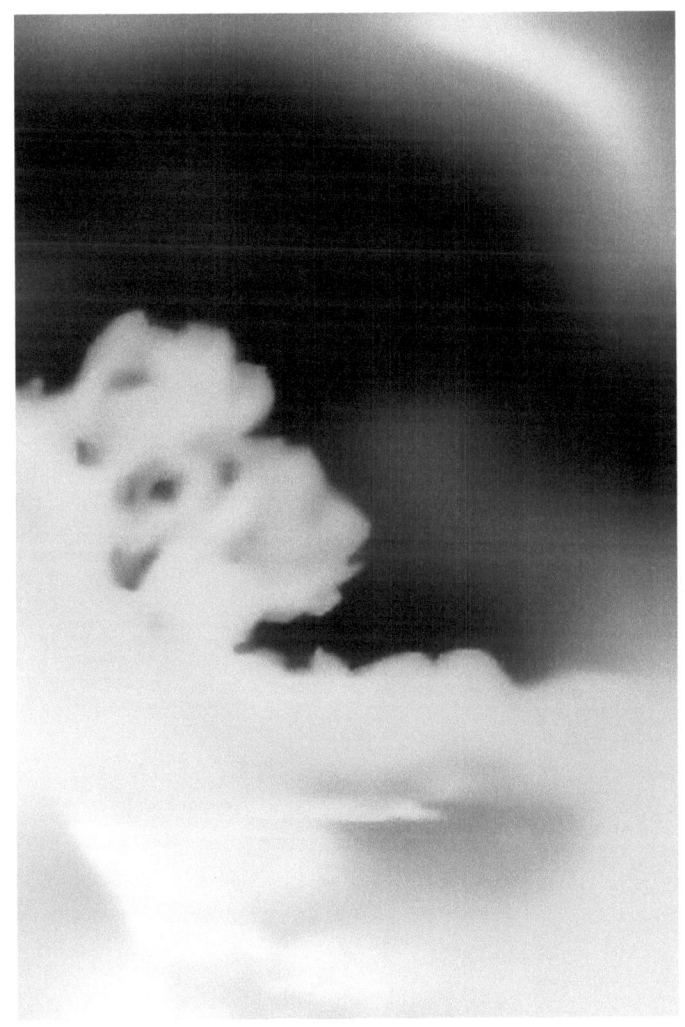

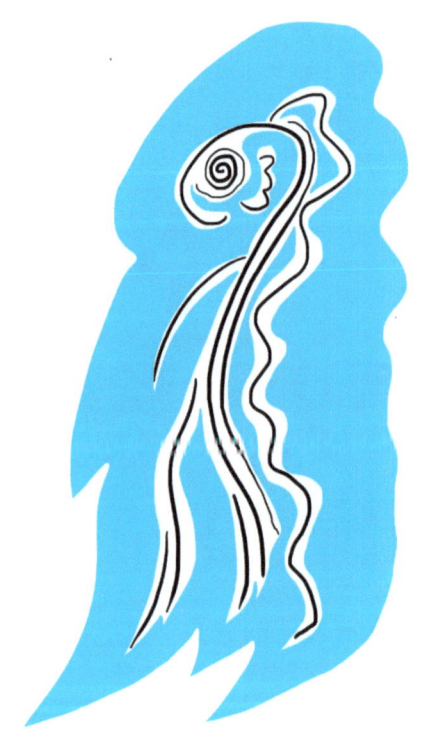

CHAPTER 5: RESILIENCE

They want to remember when they felt part of the sky.
Like water drops anchored on seafloors.
How I see is what I know.

My body will remember for me despite my oblivion.
From resilience comes binding.
We're in the Parramatta River.[1]

Where faded bodies move between two worlds.
Adaptation is salvation.
We're bearing the traces of millenarian ruptures.

Stars will fade into the oceans again.
We're becoming water.

---

1. Tobin, Leanne (2021). "Ngalawan — We Live We Remain", in *Rivus: A Glossary of Water*, op. cit., pp. 359-360.

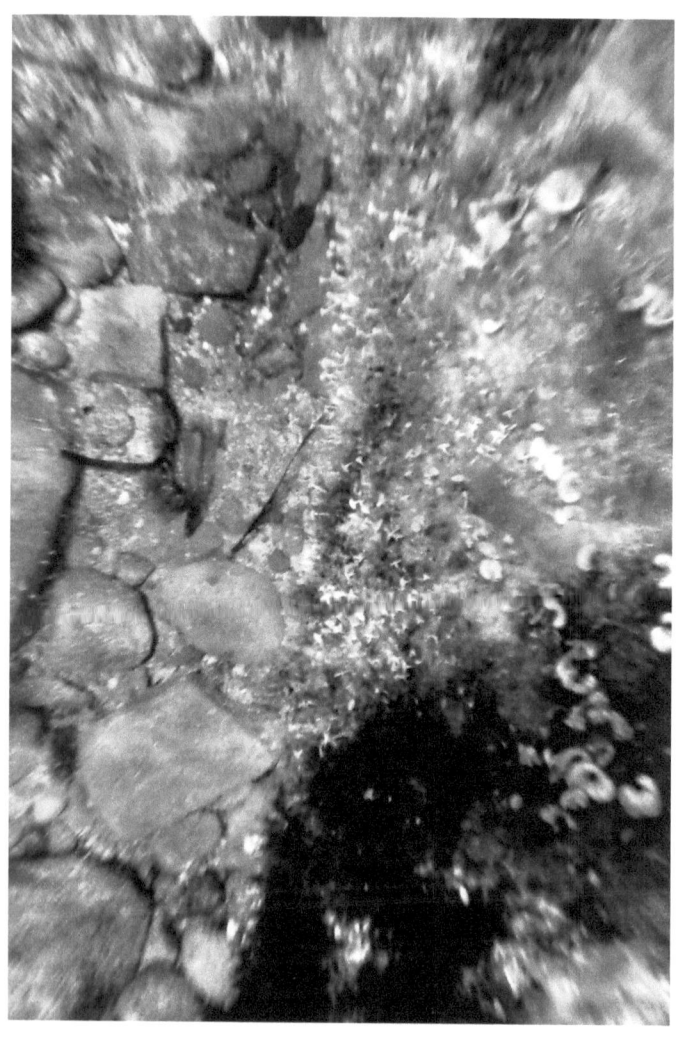

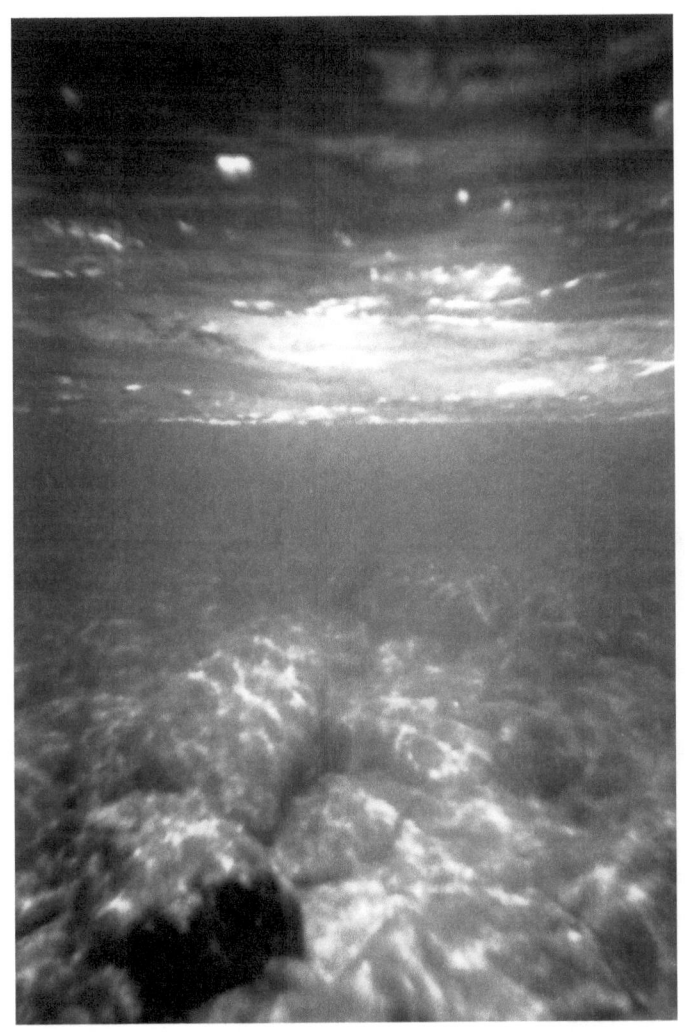

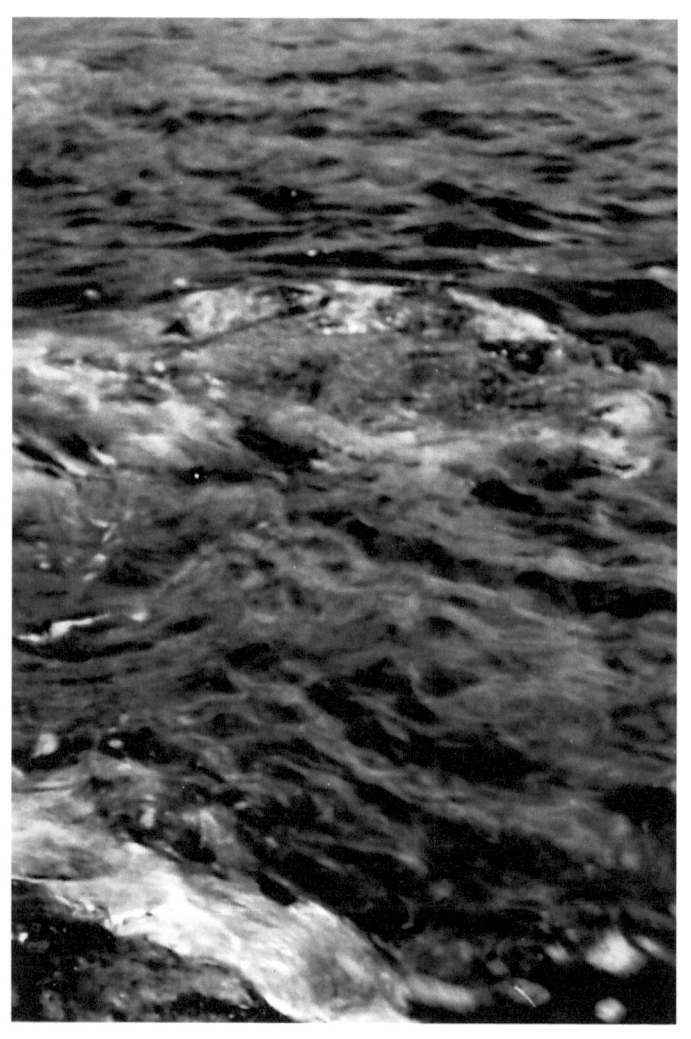

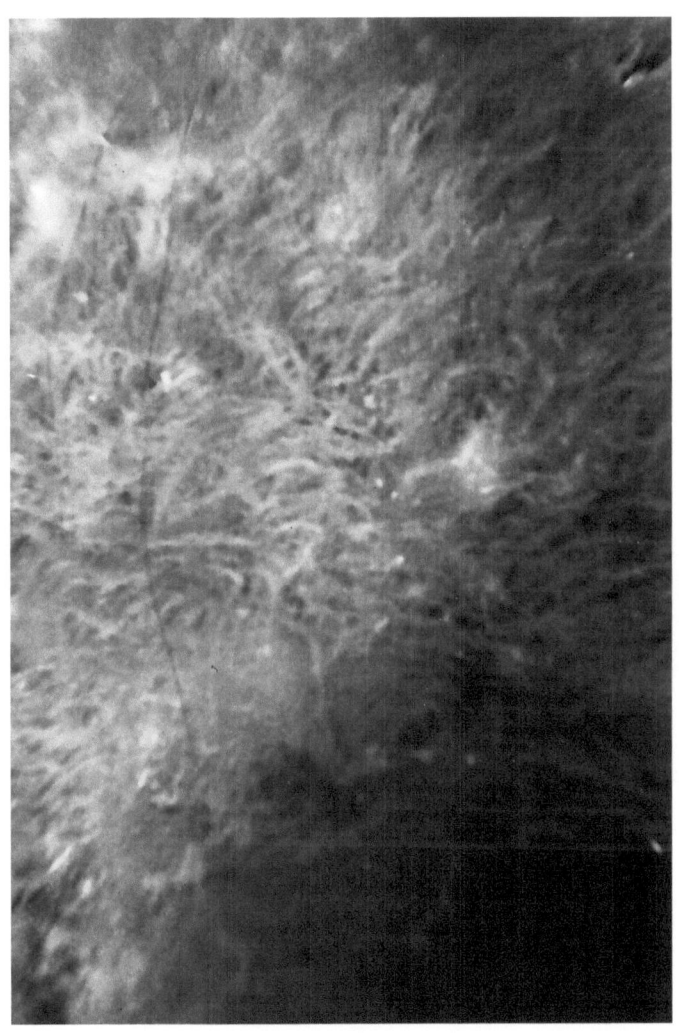

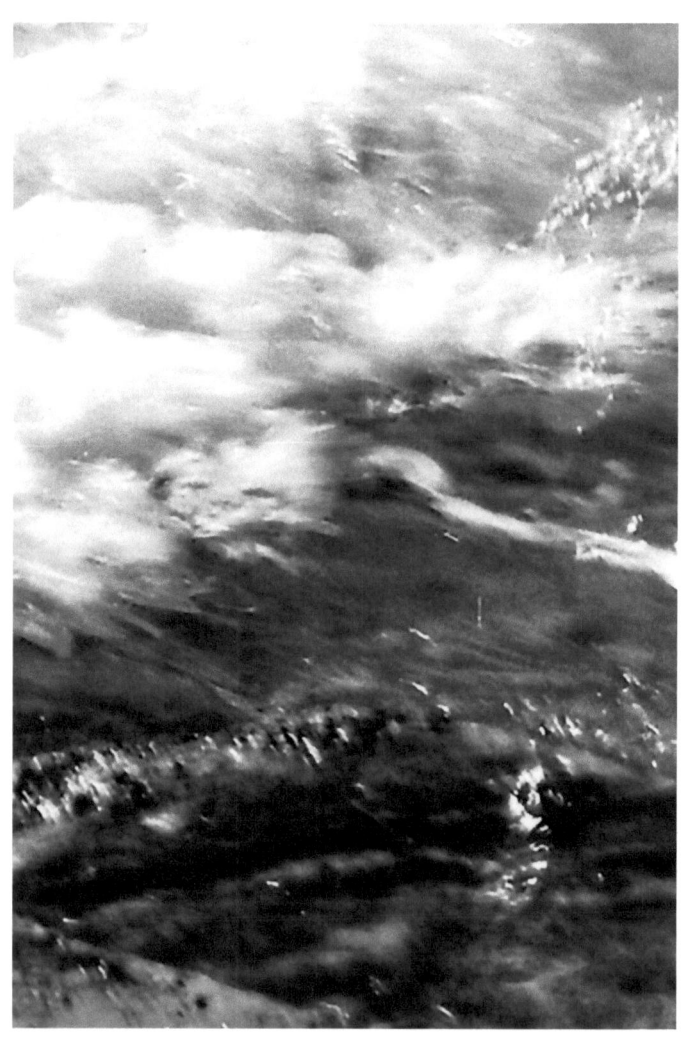

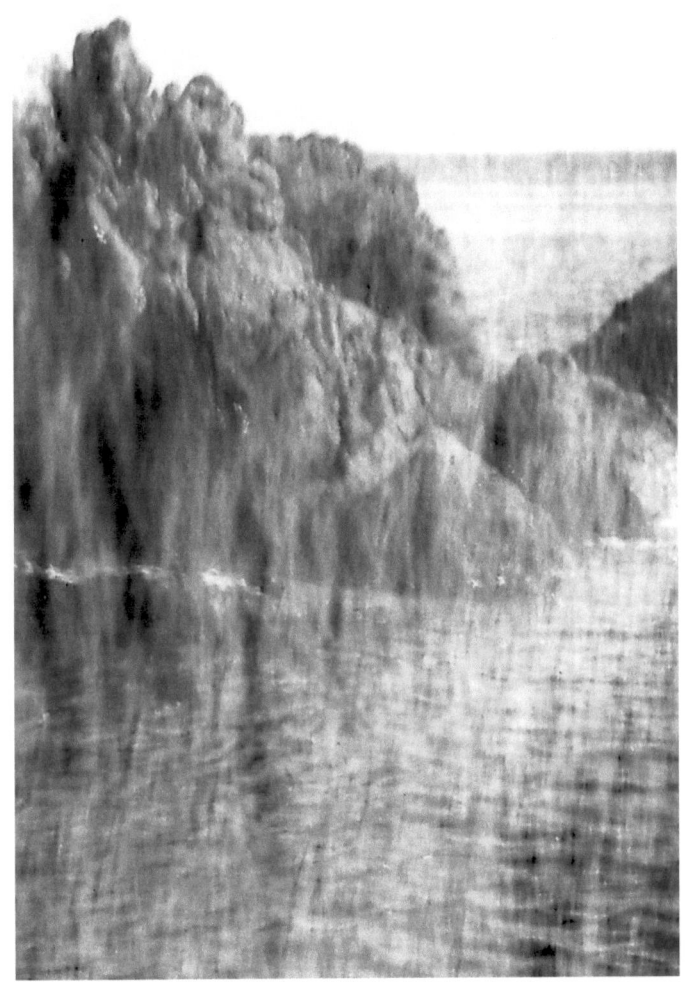

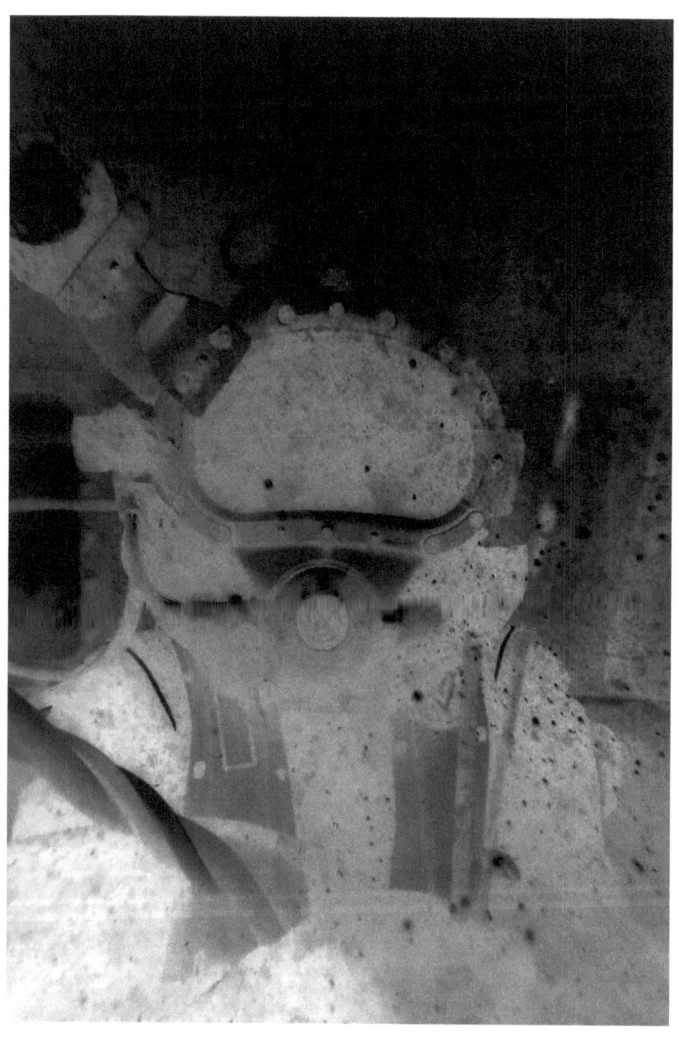

AFTERWORD: FOLLOWING THE THREAD OF WATER

27-9-23

> It is the nature of stone to be satisfied. It is the nature of water to want to be somewhere else.[1]
>
> - Mary Oliver

When legendary experimental filmmaker Stan Brakhage was dying of bladder cancer, he decided to submerge the lens of his long-neglected, though still new Bolex camera in the waters of the creek near his home in Colorado. In a self-described trance state that lasted nearly two hours, he filmed the subaquatic goings-on. The resulting work, which he edited in the days between exploratory surgery and the removal of his bladder, is titled "Commingled Containers" (1996).[2] In what would be his last movie, he specifically wanted to explore underwater friction, how the sun above illuminated the colliding of water and stone below. It's a film that reflects the process of its making, paying attention to the choreography of a human body (as an encased body of water itself) silently grinding against its own impending demise. This reflexive ocularcentric consideration of death and its relationship to underwater friction beneath an overwater sun has always made me feel uneasy, discomposed, and melancholic. In my experience, we sociologists generally avoid talking about their feelings, a trend I have always found to be rather silly, especially given what we know about the centrality

---

[1]. Oliver, Mary 2000. *VQR: A National Journal OF Literature & Discussion*. Vol. 76, No. 2 (Spring).

[2]. MacDonald, S. (2003). "The Filmmaker as Visionary: Excerpts from an Interview with Stan Brakhage." *Film Quarterly*, Vol. 56, No. 3 (Spring), pp. 2-11.

of emotion in organizing cognition, consciousness, and the making of what we know. So yes, I feel a certain dis-ease when watching Brakhage's last filmic gasp. The imagery unsettles me. In the 25 years since first seeing that film, I hadn't really seen much else like it until I received a copy of this book along with Julie's request that I consider writing the afterword for it.

I responded to that email with an enthusiastic yes and asked her to tell me more about the work. She replied, "The photographs in this book don't aim at being nice, clear, or even pretty (although some are kind of eerie)." I couldn't have agreed more. They're decidedly not nice, and many are not clear in the way we often expect photographs to be, even when they're abstract or transcendental. As for not pretty (or more simply put, ugly) … well, I may not be the best judge of that. When I first saw the images in Thread of Water, I began daydreaming not about water but rather about soil, specifically the dirt-encrusted severed ear on the manicured lawn in David Lynch's 1986 film Blue Velvet. In my mind's eye I could almost see the ants crawling as the camera worked its way gyroscopically into the fleshy canal, the landscape of the inner ear slowly becoming stranger with each additional degree of magnification and rotation (my flourish, not Lynch's). Ultimately, the ear in my inner viewfinder ended up looking quite a lot like some of the immersive photographs you've just experienced.

At the curious intersection of ethnography and art, this alchemic immersion in alternate forms can be gimmicky, which is how I tend to view much of the immersive video work that has recently been characterized as "sensory ethnography." But in theory-informed, technically proficient hands, like Julie's, the camera goes deep inside a seemingly familiar element to reveal the strangeness of things we once took for granted or just routinely ignored or never had the time or opportunity to see in this way.

When I was a child, my friends and I played a game where we inched our faces closer and closer together, to the point where the face we beheld had become something else: an abstraction, a surrealist rendering, a grotesque masquerade of itself. Relatedly, before realizing the power and efficiency of drugs to alter perception, I would often spend long periods of time squinting with varying torque or aggressively pushing my eyeballs inward in an attempt to distort my view of the world around me. These alterations invariably revealed a reality beneath the reality, a previously hidden world now conjured into existence by a manual, or chemical, stimulus. Seeing what's under there – under the surface that we typically take for granted – can be a frightening proposition. As American actor and comedian Lily Tomlin once quipped, "Reality is a crutch for people who can't cope with drugs."

Looking at or even just imagining what's under the hood can be alarming. The work of Swiss psychoanalyst C.G. Jung comes to mind. Part of me wonders if the photos here are unnerving because the imagery in them emerges from and reflects some dark precinct of the Jungian collective unconscious. Jung used the term "imago" to differentiate the objective reality of a person or a thing from the subjective perception of its meaning or importance. When we look at something or the image of that something, we form a perception of it, and that perception results from the interplay of our own biographical experience (including past traumas) and the vast array of archetypal forms in the collective unconscious. Onto the image of the object we project meaning. In this way, then, no image is innocent because, frankly, no biography is pure. Merely being alive sullies us all.

> Because of its extremely subjective origin, the imago is frequently more an image of a subjective functional complex than of the object itself. In the analytical treatment of unconscious products it is essential that the imago should not be assumed to be identical with the object; it is better to regard it as an image of the subjective relation to the object.[3]

Put in different, more Lacanian terms, whatever we look at looks back at us, and in its gaze we can see the reflection of what it's seeing, and existentially speaking, what's inside of us is often very messy.[4]

---

3. The Collected Works of C.G. Jung. 20 vols. Bollingen Series XX, translated by R.F.C. Hull, edited by H. Read, M. Fordham, G. Adler, and Wm. McGuire. Princeton University Press, Princeton, 1953-1979, p. 6, par. 812.

4. Lacan, J. *The Four Fundamental Concepts of Psycho-Analysis*. Trans. Alan Sheridan. Ed. Jacques-Alain Miller. New York: Norton, 1977, p. 92.

Beyond messiness, there's a visual anarchy in Julie's thermographic images, but it's this very agitation that suggests a new, potentially emancipatory narrative altogether, one that invokes Julie's process and consciousness, her commitment to an ethnographic ethic, and her creation of an ethnographic-artistic ethos that eschews blind empiricism. As Julie curates the experience of embodied engagement in deep waters, I as a viewer find myself also entering those waters, or rather my own facsimile of them, yet I obviously see things differently than she does. After all, either consciously or unconsciously, I own and operate my own imago. Or maybe it's the one in charge? Whatever the case, I am seeing my understanding of the matter look back at me, into me, and in its looking I see what it sees. This is my projection, which at its core destabilizes the neat and clean image of selfhood that I and most others try very hard to sustain on a daily basis. In this context of mutually generative ontological insecurity, the unanswerable question is, do our projections believe in each other?[5]

Why are the images in this book "eerie" or even "ugly," I wonder. Why are they so disquieting to me in a way that recalls my first experience seeing Brakhage's death film? Maybe they're like the Lynchian ear. On a head, it's fine, but on a lawn, it's … just … not fine. And then there's the proximity. The closer we get to something familiar, the stranger it often becomes. The scarier it often seems? Bring these two ideas together, I am getting closer and closer to something that is out of its usual place. That's disturbing.

By virtue of what these images exclude, or more precisely, what we mark as absent from them, we undergo another kind of destabilization. They challenge the viewer's sense of location in that they lack the usual geospatial contextual cues that help orient us. They're simply not anchored in what we can call a common reality. What makes these even more disruptive to the psyche is the fact that all of us, or nearly all, have been

---

5. A nod to Emerson's line, "Our moods do not believe in each other." Emerson, R.W. (1841). *Essays*. London, England: J. Fraser.

there (i.e., underwater) but we haven't been there (i.e., underwater in this way). This isn't foreign territory, exactly. It's familiar but also quite strange – because although we have been underwater, only rarely have we occupied underwater spaces long enough to begin ignoring them in the way we do our out-of-water topographies.

Temporally, too, these images are unmoored. They could have been any time. Through these images, Julie places time and space into unending suspension, which can at times feel threatening on a phenomenological level. Aside from our knowledge that thermography is a fairly recently developed technology, these images could have been made in nearly any modern epoch. Moreover, there's no firm sense of time passing or having passed. These images don't even appear to possess the capacity of passing time. By disavowing the modernist imperative to evoke a timeline, the images invite us to a state of indefinite moratorium. Oh how eerie that can feel.

Ultimately, the combining of spatial and temporal dislocation impairs the exercise of capable proprioception. The images here possess a high degree of interpellation – they, with their obvious strangeness, call out to the viewer, perforating the perceptual membrane through which everyday life conventionally appears as a blur of continuous events and indistinguishable sequences. In calling out to us unexpectedly, they induce a wobble, a stutter, a slight lurch in the stride, as when we hear someone call our name while walking down a street in a city we've never visited before. In a word, these images disrupt the way we see. In so doing they push us to see a different way, and quite possibly lose our way, if only for a bit.[6] And isn't that quite a good thing, sometimes?

Finally, there is the fact of water's materiality. When our bodies are underwater, they operate differently. As Picken and Ferguson point out, being

---

6. In this way, the images here (and images everywhere) enjoy varying potential for interrupting what we know to be "reality," which is mostly a blurry backdrop of indistinguishable forms. For this notion I owe thanks to Georg Simmel's remarkable essay: Simmel, G. (1950). "The Metropolis and Mental Life." In K. H. Wolff (Ed.), *The Sociology of Georg Simmel* (pp. 409-424). New York: The Free Press.

underwater (in their case, scuba diving), "troubles long-held notions of what it is to be human, because this existence is explicitly networked, turbid, and reshaped by the act of participating in life under water." While I have never engaged in deep water diving as a practice, I have spent considerable periods of time in the water as an open water swimmer, lifeguard, and swim instructor. To my mind, the feeling of running or trying to move quickly when submerged is the waking life counterpart to the experience of REM atonia during a nightmare, that deeply disturbing realization that you cannot move, run, fight, or scream when you're facing a terrifying element, as if you are enmired in sticky goo. The dream movement, like underwater locomotion, is labored, slow, dramatized, while the feeling propelling it is super-charged. This is the behavior of inchoate emotion. This is my own experience of buried trauma as it begins to stir itself from a deep slumber.

The bottom line is that there is no bottom. It's turtles all the way down. Switching back, I can tell you that David Lynch's film has never compelled me to go out looking for wayward body parts glistening in the summer sun. Julie's images, however, did compel me to seek out experiences that might guide me toward a new understanding of life underwater and, just maybe, life within my own consciousness. This is exactly what happened after I read this book: The water summoned me, and I went to meet it.

TOW as a Field Guide for Seeing

Initially, I intellectualized this entire project, situating Julie's work in the history of heavily positivist work in visual sociology, a small academic field she and I share. I reflected on how for many decades this field has seemed hellbent on legitimizing itself though realist photography and, more recently, documentary video.[7] Practitioners typically use rationalistic imagery as data about the world out there, not about the world in here or the world of the senses. This is predictable given the field's original

---

7. For a solid overview of the subfield and its history, see: Harper, D. (2023). *Visual Sociology*, 2nd Ed. London: Routledge.

raison d'être: self-legitimation.[8] Julie's work in this treatment calls this rationalism into question by interrogating the interior recesses of predisposition, impulse, and pre-vocal processing over the top of which the rationalist paradigm has been precariously erected. I am now seeing her work as redolent of the friction generated by the movement of water over Brakhage's stones. I would hope it behaves much like water over stone, auguring the erosion of this discipline's blind (and blindered) adherence to Western empiricism and hegemonic epistemologies.

The history of work in this subfield, much of my own included, is laden with genuflections to empiricism. Most of the work treats the image not as a datum or even expression, but rather as document, a "reality substitute."[9] Nearly all of the books published in visual sociology rely principally on text to convey their arguments and use imagery, mainly photographs, to illustrate the conceptual or analytical points they're trying to make in their studies. It's too often just tediously straightforward, if you ask me. Rarely does one encounter a published book or article that aspires to do something different, something so disruptive, something so very weird.

In itself the book as I see it is an ode to oddness, one that I really hope the field of visual sociology attempts to reckon. The confrontation she speaks of is critical. I mean, what else is human life if not odd? How often do we feel odd? Think odd thoughts? Do things that strike us, or others, as odd? Oddness is not a way of life; it IS life. One of the things she did was to provoke my own engagement with the oddness of human relationships with water. Like a skilled deconstructionist, she has pointed up the vitality of the strange, the misstep, the unspoken, the ill-formed, the seemingly accidental. The cracks in the seawall are the point of the whole concept of

---

8. This field was born of and into a legitimation crisis. A number of white male sociologists who had experience making photographs commercially or as hobbyists were trying to draw on their image-making skills in the doing of their professional work as sociologists, too often finding themselves running into resistance or, more often (and even worse), dismissal or indifference by mainstream colleagues. They wanted their work to be recognized as REAL sociology. So they banded together to share it with each other, create their own journals, and hold their own conferences. From this formative experience they began to clear a plot of territory on the periphery of mainstream sociology, calling it "visual sociology." In short, experimentalism is often quite bad for a fledgling discipline's or genre's legitimation, so the work tends to be staid in its effort to conform to convention and accepted practice.

9. Feldman, E.B. (1971). *Varieties of Visual Experience*, Basic Edition. Englewood Cliffs, NJ: Prentice-Hall, p. 435.

"seawall." After all, the crack is erosion, the ineluctable and insurmountable force that can be forestalled or slowed but never prevented, much less eradicated. I thought I was going into the world to experience water, and I did, but I think the greater, more fruitful, and more terrifying task became going into my Self.

Julie's consideration of ethnography as an ethic merits quoting here.

> My narrative begins with ethnography as an ethic. It unveils emotions like feeling weird, insecure, and trying to find one's way out of emotional confusion by constantly leaving one's comfort zone – not as an escape, but as a confrontation. It embraces doing, and experimenting along the way, to better understand what critical practice can be in the name of, without losing sight of self-distancing. It opens ways to reclaim one's body and relationship with the elements following years of emotional and physical trauma. (3)

This insight became the foundational principle in my experience of converting the book into a "field guide for seeing." When thinking about how to write this essay, and struggling mightily to arrive at a framework, I felt the water drawing me out. My apartment sits about 150 meters from the shoreline of Lake Michigan, the fourth largest lake in the world by surface area (22,300 sq. miles). Inside my home studio, I began to long for the lake. I needed to remember the gills I never had. So after slathering my consciousness with passages and images from this book and my body with sunscreen, I ventured into the maritime summer days of the coastal community I call home with a nascent desire to seek out images I hadn't thought to seek out before, images that didn't yet exist because I hadn't yet opened my mind to the possibility of formulating them. Equipped with this book's material, I was ready to edit the imago.

Membrane Logic: Fluidity and Porosity

On the first day of my many daily trips into "the field," I carried with me an insight from one of the references in Julie's text, the hydrofeminist scholar Astrida Neimanis:

The coast is only a 'line' if you pull the aperture out; in this way, you artificially fix it as a 'line'. The line is a snapshot that extracts the coast from the flow of time where it cannot be weathered or eroded. But in a thickness of time, the line is actually a blur. The line is a zone in which things happen. Passage, transition, becoming, transmogrification: these are the labours of the coastal zone.[10]

Every physical boundary expresses, implies, or reinforces a social process. The reverse also holds. I can't think of a single social process that doesn't involve the production of at least one physical boundary. This principle, and its corollary, has served as my jumping off point as a documentary filmmaker, sociologist, and artist. Yet I began to realize just how fluid this particular boundary is, this "dividing line" between water and land. There are suspensions and slippages, though they're all still shaped or undergirded by prevailing social conventions. What I often in my life have uncritically called "the shoreline," I realized, isn't a line at all. It's a porous membrane, and not just physically but socially, too.

In a coastal zone, maritime sociology can bear fascinating fruit. One of the key insights of sociology relates to the power of the situation in shaping human behavior. The physical composition of the environment matters greatly when it comes to how we behave. When people are near, and especially when they are in, water, they most often dress differently, do different things, say different words, move their bodies differently. We know the coastal zone is a zone if only because at a certain distance from the waterline, carrying a surfboard down the street becomes a strange sight to see. Social and cultural life – norms, customs, mores, rituals, roles, etc. – are slightly different in this membrane area, this transitional zone of water and land. There's lamentably little visual research or artistic work on the behavior of humans in relation to the behavior of water.[11] This is un

---

10. Bezan, S. & Neimanis, A. (2022). "Hydrofeminism on the Coastline: An Interview with Astrida Neimanis," *Anthropocenes – Human, Inhuman, Posthuman* 3(1). DOI: https://doi.org/10.16997/ahip.1363

11. Notable exceptions include two books and an early journal article: Edgerton, R.B. (1979). *Alone Together: Social Order on an Urban Beach*; Osbaldiston, N. (2017). *Towards a Sociology of the Coast: Our Past, Present and Future Relationship to the Shore*; Poole, M. (1981). "Maritime sociology: towards a delimation of themes and analytical frameworks," *Maritime Policy & Management*, 8:4, 207-222.

fortunate, especially given the fact that humans are bodies of water themselves. The Thread of Water has inspired me to make ethnographic forays into this transitional coastal zone in which I live and to begin developing a series of aqueous ontologies, ways of seeing and understanding the world with water at the center and flowing everlastingly in every direction.

Immersion, Abstraction, and the Death of Always Knowing

Developing this book into a field guide for seeing helped me, as an ethnographer and visual artist, to extend myself well beyond seeing. By applying its principles and insights and images to the careful study of my own existence in/of water, I came to understand more clearly just how much murk there is down below. Where I always assumed bedrock, I now encounter a shifting layer of silt pocked with bedeviling slurries of primordial tendencies. The scaffolding of my "scholarly" and "professional" self once stood but now wobbles atop this floating slab. While some may find such a realization to be a real horror show, I find myself strangely liberated by it. I am a little more capable now than I was before I read this book of figuring out how to see inside myself a little more clearly, a necessary procondition for seeing out there a little more clearly. As Julie states above, "… water bears consciousness and the promises of cosmic connection." Therein lies hope. The hope of going beyond seeing and documenting and analyzing and otherwise perpetrating conceptual violence on the world out there. The hope of pursuing the experience of emotion, feeling, impulse, intuition, and hunches as neurochemically concocted and socially inflected undercurrents that serve as wellsprings of knowing, of being, of practice. I think this development can engender the highest stakes conversations in all of social science and is therefore the most vital of issue facing ethnography as a method, an ethic, and way of living.

I will close this afterword with an excerpt from the collection of field notes I amassed while making this book part of my life practice. Nearly every night at 9 pm, shortly after sunset, I walk to the lake. I am typically alone out there. On this night, I say my notes into an audio recorder:

Tonight I am in the lake for what's probably the last night swim of the year. Tomorrow the temperature will drop and most likely it won't come back. The air tonight is warm. The sky is overcast. The combination of the dark water and the overcast sky makes the horizon nearly indiscernible. I swim out past the buoys, to a point where I can no longer touch the bottom, even when I try my hardest at diving down as far as I can, holding my breath as long as possible, staying deep for as long as possible. Down here it's pitch dark. I have lost my sense of myself. My bearings aren't correct. I am out of breath and involuntarily begin to inhale, it's all water. I come up gasping for air, choking on water I didn't mean to ingest, vomiting from my mouth and out my nose while treading water, realizing only now just how alone I am. It's just me and water, in water, as water. The panic vanishes suddenly, and I'm left with the calmest calamitous vision of my life: dying here and now. I think that would be just fine. I would go where I'm wanted, anyway, and with very little … displacement. The gulls are gulling, but I don't know what they're saying. The mist is misting, but it's nowhere close to raining. The wind is wind-ing, but it's warmth suggests another thing entirely. Soon it'll be time to return, and I hope it's on a night like this, in this lake or a lake very much like this. It would be okay to journey home now. On the wings of a tiny death arrives the promise of even more beautiful ways and days to come. Moliere once wrote, "we die only once, but for such a long time." I used to believe this, but now I'm not so sure. Maybe there's room in this life for a thousand (or more) little deaths. Without them, there might not be enough hope to go on. Thank you, Julie.

Now let us go, like water, elsewhere.

Greg Scott
Chicago, IL 2023

… we, too, are made
of water, of vast and beckoning seas.[12]

- Ada Limón

---

12. Limón, A. (2023). "In Praise of Mystery: a Poem for Europa." Retrieved from the Library of Congress, https://www.loc.gov/programs/poetry-and-literature/poet-laureate/poet-laureate-projects/a-poem-for-europa/

www.ingramcontent.com/pod-product-compliance
Lightning Source LLC
Chambersburg PA
CBHW040319220526
45473CB00009B/2490